Palaces of Venice

There is nothing more precious than peace; nothing else is able to ensure more happiness to human beings. The peace is the essential introduction for the progress of the humanity.

Daisaku Ikeda
President Soka Gakkai International SGI

Andrea Fasolo

Palaces of Venice

Photography
Mark E. Smith

arsenale e✝ editrice

Andrea Fasolo

Palaces of Venice

Photography
Mark E. Smith

Translation
Emblema s.a.s. di Valerio Galeazzi

Print
EBS Editoriale Bortolazzi Stei,
Verona

Second Edition
May 2004

Arsenale Editrice
A division of EBS
Via Monte Comun, 40
37057 San Giovanni Lupatoto (Vr)
www.arsenale.it
arsenale@arsenale.it

ISBN 88-7743-294-2

Contents

Introduction	7
Ca' Corner della Regina	14
Ca' d'Oro	16
Ca' Da Mosto	22
Ca' Dario	24
Ca' Dolfin Manin	28
Ca' Foscari	30
Ca' Pesaro	34
Ca' Rezzonico	38
Ca' Tron	44
Ca' Zenobio	46
Casa Torres	50
Fondaco dei Turchi	52
Palazzo Albrizzi	56
Palazzo Ariani	58
Palazzo Balbi	60
Palazzo Barbaro	62
Palazzo Belloni Battagia	64
Palazzo Bembo	68
Palazzo Bernardo	70
Palazzo dei Camerlenghi	72
Palazzo Centani	74
Palazzo Coccina Tiepolo Papadopoli	76
Palazzo Contarini del Bovolo	78
Palazzo Contarini delle Figure	80
Palazzo Contarini Fasan	84
Palazzo Contarini Dal Zaffo	86
Palazzo Corner della Ca' Granda	88
Palazzo Corner Loredan Piscopia	90
Palazzo Corner-Mocenigo	92
Palazzo Corner Spinelli	94
Palazzo Correr Contarini Zorzi	98
Palazzo d'Anna	100
Palazzo Dandolo	102
Palazzo Falier Canossa	104
Palazzo Giustinian	108
Palazzo Giustinian Lolin	110
Palazzo Giustinian Morosini	112
Palazzo Grassi	114
Palazzo Grimani	118
Palazzo Grimani Marcello	122
Palazzo Gussoni Cavalli Franchetti	124
Palazzo Gussoni Grimani Della Vida	128
Palazzo Labia	130
Palazzo Loredan dell'Ambasciatore	136
Palazzo Loredan Vendramin Calergi	138
Palazzo Mastelli del Cammello	142
Palazzo Michiel delle Colonne	144
Palazzo Mocenigo Casa Nuova	146
Palazzo Mocenigo Casa Vecchia	150
Palazzo Moro-Lin	152
Palazzo Morosini Brandolini	154
Palazzo Morosini Sagredo	156
Palazzo Pesaro degli Orfei, Fortuny	162
Palazzo Pisani	168
Palazzo Pisani Gritti	170
Palazzo Pisani Moretta	174
Palazzo Priuli all'Osmarin	180
Palazzo Priuli Ruzzini	182
Palazzo Querini Benzon	184
Palazzo Soranzo	186
Palazzo Soranzo van Axel	188
Palazzo Venier dei Leoni	192
Bibliography	*197*

Introduction

If we think of architecture as a "creation which cannot be separated from civil life and the society in which it manifests itself" (A. Rossi), the exceptional integrity of the urban fabric of Venice which has survived to the present day makes the city a true "urban adventure"(F. Posocco). Monuments and buildings become a sign of a collective will which finds in architecture the stimulus for the realisation of appropriate structures and spaces to fulfil the daily needs of its inhabitants and which only later becomes a demonstration of aesthetic intentions.

Therefore it is easy to understand that the characteristics of Venice have always had a fundamental role in distinguishing the city from all others.

The origins of the city date back to the period between the 5th and 7th centuries, when Barbarian invasions devastated the north of Italy, forcing the population which normally lived in highlands to find shelter in the wetlands of the Venetian lagoon.

Thus water became the natural and vital element for the people, who organised themselves into communities and appreciated the value of developing their activities by con-

Pages 6-7: view of Canal Grande from the loggia of Ca' d'Oro.

centrating and consolidating settlements with exemplary wisdom and prudence.

Environmental conditions, a changing equilibrium and tireless work in order to win over the land from the sea determined the nature of a society made up of non absolute hierarchies and of an autonomous economy based on commerce.

Today Venice is made up of 118 small islands, linked together by four hundred bridges and crossed by 160 canals.

In 697 the election of the first Doge established the beginning of the Venetian Republic.

During the following centuries the urban structure developed, firstly with the construction of mainly wooden buildings on land consolidated through the planting of piles with an overlying stone base; the most important brick constructions were constructed for the bishop's office on the island of Olivo-Castello and for the Doge's office, with church alongside, in the area that still exists today.

Only after the 11th century, following the development of its role in the Mediterranean and of commerce with distant lands, were the warehouses filled with all kinds of rare and precious merchandise, leading to the promotion of urban services, road links and intensive building along the banks of the Canal Grande around Rialto, the economic centre of the city.

The houses with associated courtyard facing on to the canals – which were the main communications network – fulfilled all the functional needs in terms of workplace, warehouses, stables and housing, giving rise to a type of structure and arrangement which was legitimised over the years: the Venetian warehouse.

Its layout was the object of architectural experimentation in these first centuries, producing a wide range of solutions which centred on a tripartite set up , with an atrium linked to the water-door and the land-door, with the warehouses and courtyard at the sides and a central room on the first floor, leading off to the residential accommodation and offices (the *pórtego*). The wall delimiting the building overlooking the canal became the façade, a buffer without any structural function which overlooked the water with recurring features represented by a porch on the ground floor for loading and unloading and a continuous gallery on the upper floor. The severe decoration was entrusted to arches with tall abutments, plain stone features and finely-worked stone on Byzantine or Romanesque themes.

Architectural design, which was increasingly conditioned by urban and aesthetic requirements, taking the architecture away from its original function, took on increasing importance, marking the whole period starting from the 14th century to the end of the 15th century.

The political and economical decision to become a territorial-continental state, due to the reduction of the strategic and commercial role in the Mediterranean led to an improvement in living conditions and a notable increase in the population (almost one hundred thousand inhabitants). The resulting increase in building involved the exploitation of useful areas, the recovery of the river-bed of the canals and the resettlement of existing structures, with the object of establishing continuity in terms of construction, the façade of the building having considerable importance, mainly from an aesthetic point of view. The typical structural characteristics remained almost unchanged: the courtyard was reduced, although it retained its dynamic function,

while the atrium and the pòrtego on the first floor still remained the central axis of the whole building. The façade became a spectacular element, sometimes eclectic and unconstrained, which availed itself of the experience of previous centuries in order to offer innovative figurative expressions. Hence the introduction of large windows, either single or multiple light, the decorative fervour of the Venetian arch, first gothic trefoil and subsequently the introduction of quatrefoil, the changes in the corners of the fine smooth or twisted columns, the floor decoration and the dentate cornices, the stone cladding, the marble decoration and the paintings. All these elements led to the front wall losing its structural importance and reducing itself to a simple linear framework.

The florid gothic style appears to reach its culmination towards the end of the 15th century with the realisation of the Palazzo Ducale, indeed one can note the first signs of humanistic and renaissance influence on architecture which was to bring Venice to its cultural climax in the 16th century.

Jacopo de' Barbari's bird's eye view of 1500, shows Venice to be almost at saturation point in terms of

space, at the beginning of the political and economic difficulties linked to the growth of neighbouring territorial powers and the reduction of its strategic and commercial role in the Mediterranean, whose importance was by then undermined by the discovery of the new world and of new routes for the Orient.

Despite this, the references, operators and models continued to extend as a result of utopian requirements and due to the individual ambitions of the great aristocratic families, which ignored the recommendations of the Higher Council, which requested reserve and sobriety.

The new requirements for showiness were mainly evident in the monumental nature of the buildings and in the façades facing onto the waterfront, with evident results. This is the case of Ca' Vendramin Calergi, designed by the Como architect Codussi. Truly majestic, the Palazzo is a typical example of an unconscious framework of reference for all the monumental and oversized buildings which nevertheless do not succeed in achieving recognition as "Venetian" and do not influence in an incisive way the evolution of residential city architecture. This is also the case of the private architecture of Jacopo Sansovino, an architect from Rome who, departing from pre-existing architecture, proposed a magnificence never attempted before, for public buildings alone, by making it into the "art of the state" (M. Tafuri).

If we consider the wounds caused by the plague in 1630, the following century is remarkable for the creativity of the works of Baldassarre Longhena who managed to combine perfectly the solidity of the structure with 'chiaroscuro' effects and the richness of mouldings and decoration. The city did not expand further, but extensive restoration was carried out, a sign of the strong wish for renewal and of a rejuvenated *joie de vivre*. Together with the architecture, stucco craftsmen, painters, decorators and carpenters who celebrated the rich aristocratic families in the precious and virtuosos interiors of the Palazzi contributed towards the creation of Venice, which still today fascinates the visitor precisely because it is so "excessive", always at the limits of regulations and planning controls.

By the beginning of the 18th century, Venice appeared once again to have gained artistic primacy but ironically political and economical decadence advanced implacably with the birth of the Rococò style. "On a horizon without a future, which appeared to be pervaded with widespread and imminent sense of ultimate representation " (G. Romanelli) the by now rare Venetian architecture of Giorgio Massari, Domenico Rossi and Andrea Tirali stands out, supported by intensive activity to recover and restore the interiors, which were furnished with sublime and shabby charm represented by stucco decoration, chandeliers, paintings, crystal, porcelain, lacquer-work and *trompe-l'œil*.

The neo-classical period marks the epilogue of the Venetian Republic, which in 1797, was indeed finally to fall, carried away by the Napoleonic movement.

The "most city-like city that exists" (Sergio Bettini) with its inability to conform and the unshakeable strength which has always characterised it from its very origin, today appears to lack energy, finding itself at the mercy of the environment and social-economic difficulties, unable to find opportunities for renewal and development, neglected in terms of economic interests and relying on mass tourism which is considered the last resource.

However, "the hope for a new equilibrium is still alive, on the basis of adequate intervention linked to the external environment, enabling this extraordinary demonstration of human ingenuity to continue living and to keep its message of civilisation alive" (J. Fasolo).

Particular of Jacopo de' Barbari's bird's eye view of 1500: the presence of Neptune celebrates and confirms the marine power Serenissima.

Pages 12-13: the clutch of Cannaregio canal seen from Canal Grande. On the left side Palazzo Labia.

AEQVORA VENS
PORTV RESIDEO
HIC NEPTVNVS

Ca' Corner della Regina

The old gothic Palazzo of the Corner family, as it appears in the plan of Jacopo De Barbari, was destroyed at the beginning of the 18th century.

It was reconstructed on the same site, marking the construction of what is today considered to be one of the last examples of imposing palaces along the Canal Grande.

The fame of the Palazzo is due to Caterina, who was born in Venice in 1454, marrying Giacomo II of Lusingano, King of Cyprus at the age of thirteen.

In July 1473 the king died and Caterina became the new queen.

After the king's death there was a conspiracy to pass the kingdom to the illegitimate children of Giacomo. Venice took action in favour of Caterina, not just to defend a woman who had been adopted by the Venetian Republic as a daughter, an honour never before granted to a woman, but also because of the strategic importance of the kingdom of Cyprus.

On 6 June 1489 Caterina gave up the kingdom, although she conserved her titles and her royal prerogatives.

She was welcome to Venice by Doge Agostino Barbarico, from whom she received dominion of the city of Asolo in Marca Trevigiana. For almost thirty years the small and refined court of Asolo became the new kingdom of Caterina.

It was animated by artists and literary figures, among whom the scholar Pietro Bembo, who recalled the queen in the dialogue "Gli Asolani". Caterina returned to Venice definitively around the 16th century, in order to avoid the conflict which saw the Venetian Republic in contrast with the Cambrai league.

In 1510, she died in the Palazzo on the Canal Grande where she had received the "Bel Mondo" so sumptuously. In the first decade of the 18th century, the long and complicated events of the palace seemed to reach their conclusion. On 10 May 1724 the Corner brothers decided to rebuild their residence, according to a design by Domenico Rossi from Marcote.

In 1726 the façade was constructed making use of the usual stylistic components, adopted however according to proportions which were extended in terms of height. A tall and disproportionate base with monotonous ashlar-work which not even the large masks succeed in interrupting supports the two upper floors. Ca' Pesaro influenced the construction of this palazzo, as can be seen in the punctuation of the projecting columns and in the continuous balcony which runs around the side, while on the second balcony the architect instead introduced "modern" windows with sober triangular tympanums, a neo-classical feature, repressed by the powerful projecting Corinthian columns which still follow a 17th century pattern.

The extended façade section is reintroduced in the main entrance, where the sumptuous porch is situated, the columns being distributed in such a way as to play with perspective, a feature which is without precedent in the local tradition.

Two symmetrical staircases lead up to the higher floors, passing through halls: the "Porteghi" halls which face onto the Canal Grande and the courtyard. They were set out so as to minimise the extended effect resulting from the longitudinal arches decorated with copious polychrome plasterwork and frescoes.

In the interior there is trompe-l'oeil decoration by Domenico Fossati and frescoes by Costantino Cedini, painted between 1773 and 1783, glorifying the Corner family. The palazzo remained the property of the Corner family until the death of Caterino Corner in 1800, when the palace passed to Pope Pio VII, who donated the palace to the Cavansi friars.

The municipality of Venice then bought it from the Cavansi friars and turned it in to the central office of the Monte Di Pietà, while in 1971 it was taken over by the Cassa di Risparmio bank. For many years it was home to the offices of the Venice Biennial exhibition, which prepared "the Historical Contemporary Arts Archive", which is today to be found in Mestre.

The majestic eighteenth century façade of Domenico Rossi.

Ca' d'Oro

This palace is considered to be the most important example of florid gothic style along the Canal Grande. Ca' d'Oro took its name (the Golden House) from the bright, multicoloured and gilded red and blue decoration, which has unfortunately been lost, which exalted the rich decoration of the façade. This, divided horizontally and closed with coupled spiral columns at the sides and by a coping along the eaves, is completely clad with prestigious coloured marble which cancelled "the material nature of the laterite structure". The façade, which is clearly divided in two by the 13th century vertical frame, "is transformed into a poetry of contrast" (E. Concina): the light and shadow effect of the arcades along the superimposed open galleries, and the powerful sculptural features of the openwork quatrefoil on the left side is contrasted with the flat surfaces and the elaborate graphic decoration on the right-hand side. Commissioned by the rich Venetian merchant Marino Contarini, the palace was built between 1421 and 1443, on the pre-existing

palace of Ca' Zeno. The architects responsible for the work were the Lombard Matteo Raverti and the Venetians Giovanni and Bartolomeo Bon, supported by skilled craftsmen who were already working at Palazzo Ducale site. The layout in 14th century style recalls the typical example of the Fondaco palazzo, with its long atrium on the ground floor, facing onto the warehouse, which was linked by the internal courtyard to the Canal Grande; the façade facing over the canal was created by the Bon architects, with the traditionally Venetian – Byzantine use of five arches, with a wider central pointed arch, in accordance with the traditional pattern, while the upper floors have wide open galleries typical of the era and clearly inspired by the Palazzo Ducale, created by Raverti. In 1454 Marino Contarini died, and Ca' d'Oro passed to his son Pietro who died in 1469, leaving the palazzo to his two daughters, Contarina and Lucia. The palace was handed down over several generations and was initially rented out. In 1791 it was divided and

The gothic façade of the Golden House Ca' d'Oro.

A particular of the rich decoration of Ca' d'Oro façade.

ultimately it was abandoned, leading to its inevitable decay. The building has indeed been described as a "ruined asset".

In the middle of the 19th century, the prince of Russia, Alessandro Trubetzkoi who had been exiled to Siberia as a conspirator, bought the palace, and presented it to the "Divine" Maria Taglioni, who saved him by interceding with Tsar Nicolas I as a mediator.

This famous prima ballerina was truly a collector of historical palaces. In addition to this palace she also owned the Giustinian Lolin and the Corner Spinelli on the Canal grande.

She employed the engineer Giovanni Battista Meduna to restore Ca' d'Oro. As a result of a free interpretation of the gothic architecture, the intervention was disastrous, radically altering both the layout and the façade.

In 1894 the palace was acquired by Baron Giorgio Franchetti and was carefully restored. He returned the palace to its former splendour and recovered the parts which had been removed and sold. In the interior courtyard the suspended stairway was reconstructed on pointed arches and the magnificent well curb by Bartolomeo Bon sited in the centre decorated

with the figures of Charity, Justice and Fortitude, certainly a homage to the virtues of Marino Contarini. Like Contarini, Franchetti was totally devoted to the recovery of the building. He also gathered together an art collection which he left to the Italian state when he died in 1922.

Today transformed into a museum, the Franchetti gallery houses a very rich art collection partially prepared by the architect Carlo Scarpa, where in addition to the *San Sebastiano* by Andrea Mantegna, it is also possible to admire masterpieces by Pisanello and Gentile Bellini.

San Sebastiano of Andrea Mantenga placed in a sixteenth century's marble aedicule and valorized from the twentieth century restoration of Carlo Scarpa.

Ca' Da Mosto

The palace is perhaps the most beautiful example of Venetian – Byzantine architecture in the city. It belonged to the Da Mosto's family of seafarers, the most famous of whom was Alvise. In the middle of the 15th century, at the age of twenty-two, he left on board of a merchant ship, at San Vincenzo he met Prince Henry of Portugal who entrusted him the command of a ship, with which he explored the western coast of Africa for the following seven years.

The original structure of the palace was modified by the raising of the building respectively in the 17th and 18th century over the 13th century building , from which the arched architrave, the carved foliage in the arcades and the tall, smooth pillars of the water gate remain, contrasting with the upper floor, as they reflect an older style.

An innovative feature of the façade is undoubtedly the pinnacle of the arch, inserted in the round arch of the windows on the upper floor. Furthermore the large seven lancet window, (one lancet is today closed up) alongside two single lancet windows is embellished with an upper band covered with marble tessere carrying the decorative elements made up of paterae, panels, crosses and raceme friezes; the complex and originally multicoloured bestiary on either side of a Christ issuing his blessing from a throne is of remarkable quality.

The Mosto family died out at the end of the 16th century. The registry of 1661 mentions the Inn "Al Leone Bianco" which in the era must have been considered one of the most well known and luxurious Venetian hotels; its most famous guests included Emperor Joseph II – who stayed there in 1769 and 1775 – and Grand Duke Paul Petrovic, the son of Catherine II and the future Tsar, Paul I, and his consort Maria Feodorovna, for whom the Venetian nobility gave parties and laid on shows which were among the most sumptuous in the 18th century. The current state of decay and abandon of the palazzo is today the object of much controversy.

The Venetian-Byzantine façade on Canal Grande.

Ca' Dario

Giovanni Dario was born in Crete. He was a senior diplomat in Constantinople and on his return to Venice in 1484 he was hailed as a result of the peace agreement concluded with Emperor Mahomet II of the Ottoman Empire, an agreement which succeeded in satisfying the Venetian Republic, despite the serious losses suffered during sixteen years of war.

The success of the delicate diplomatic mission was rewarded by the Sultan with the gift of three woven gold robes and a substantial sum of money, while Dario was also rewarded by Venice with a property in Novanto Padova.

With the money that he received, Giovanni purchased the gothic palace on the Canal Grande, which

Above: the entrance-hall on the ground floor.

Opposite: the façade on the Canal Grande attributed to Pietro Lombardo.

was restored in 1487, becoming a part of the narrow circle of owners of palaces along the "Canalazzo".

Isolated on all four sides, and with a narrow façade, less than the length of a gondola, the palazzo reflects "at the same time both the courtly renaissance of Roman grandeur and evidence of continuity in relation to the more recent Veneto – Byzantine past" (E. Concina) Pietro Lobardo was principally responsible for the work, above all for the opulence of the cladding in green porphyry, smooth granite and coloured cut stone, decorated with discs, wheels and interwoven motifs, the building certainly represents a unique example in terms of the extensive decoration.

The compositional arrangement abandons the traditional tripartite system for a different arrangement with a three lancet on the left and a wing on the right, where the only full walls are the three squares, one on each floor, clad in marble. The renaissance windows also continue around the corner to form a sort of corner gallery, a feature which was used in gothic era today they have been walled up as a result of problems of stability.

On the death of Giovanni, the building was inherited by his daughter, the wife of Vincenzo Barbaro and remained in the family until the beginning of the 19th century.

In 1838 it was sold to Marquis Abdoll Radon Lubback Brown, a friend of Ruskin, who financed the first restoration work.

It was subsequently acquired by Count Sigismondo Zichy and then by Countess De La Baume. In 1904 the palace was subjected to major restoration work.

The need to reinforce the structure led to the removal of the façade, which was scrupulously reconstructed according to the original, with the exception of the insertion of the 19th century

iron balcony and some marble discs, the base in Istria stone, with a wealth of mouldings and on which there is the inscription 'urbis genio joannes darius', requested by Giovanni.

Sinister events that which have taken place recently involving the palace's owners have also given the palazzo a certain tragic notoriety.

Indeed, around 1970 Count Filippo Giordano Delle Lanze was murdered by his lover inside the rooms of the building, while in 1981 the musical manager Cristopher

Lambert died a violent death. Raul Gardini, who had purchased the palace from Fabrizio Ferrari, whom had suffered a financial crash, committed suicide, apparently as a result of legal investigations connected to "tangentopoli", an investigation into corruption.

Opposite: the marble great staircase that leads to noble floors.

Above: decorative particular of the façade.

Ca' Dolfin Manin

Palazzo Dolfin – Manin rises up on the site of a pre-existing complex of modest buildings, representing a "magnificence of conception, a substantial departure from pre – existing concepts [...] presenting a freedom of manoeuvre unthinkable up to that moment" (G. Romanelli) who associates it with Palazzo Corner della Ca' Granda which was constructed almost simultaneously. In 1536 the project was commissioned from Jacopo Sansovino by the magistrate of San Marco, Giovanni Dolfin, whose nickname was "dolphin" as result of an ancestor's famous swimming ability.

A wide portico with six arcades resting on pillars, the ground floor being used for storage, acts as the foundation for the two upper floors, marked by the continuous balcony and the central mullioned window. From the testimony of Francesco Sansovino and Vasari it appears that the internal courtyard, rather than the façade, was the object of wonder as a result of the extent and lightness of the composition, "in the Roman manner"

unfortunately destroyed during modernisation work at the end of the 18th century. The architectural interest was increased by the splendid performances which were given here by the 'Companie della Calza, a group of young Venetian nobleman, whom delighted in presenting shows, jokes and entertainment.

Palladio would appear to have created a "very rich scene like a town, with beautiful columns and perspectives which were truly admirable", built within the Dolfin courtyard, where a tragedy was represented, remaining for long in the memory of the spectators. In 1602 the family Dolfin died out completely, although their importance and their historic role, the family having produced a Doge, five cardinals and various important figures within the Venetian Republic, has undoubtedly been conserved within the city's culture. The palace was immediately divided among their heirs and rented out to several wealthy families.

Only at the beginning of the eighteenth century was the rich Manin family from Friuli able to reassemble the overall

unity of the palace. In 1708 some big art collectors appear to have rearranged and furnished the interior in a sumptuous manner, with paintings by Giovanni di Udine and Andrea del Sarto, rich velvets, exquisite furniture and wall coverings in golden drape, damask and tapestries designed by Raffaello.

In 1787 Ludovico Manin, the last Doge of Venice, bought the whole palace and assigned restoration work to the architect Selva. This work concluded in 1801, the palace having been completely rebuilt, with the exception of the façade, which remained the same. The interior of the palace and the courtyard were modified, according to a more organised layout.

The family Manin continued living in the palace until 1867; it then became the property of the National Bank, and today it is the main head office of the Bank of Italy.

The façade of the palace designed by Jacopo Sansovino.

Ca' Foscari

In the San Pantalon district, where the "Canalazzo" reaches a bend, a warehouse belonging to Bernardo Giustinian was constructed which was known as "the two towered house". The Republic had bought it in 1429 in order to give it as a gift, first to Gianfranco Gonzaga and subsequently, following a political U-tun of the Lord of Mantua, to Francesco Sforza. In 1452 the palace was auctioned and bought by Francesco Folcari, who ordered that it be rebuilt in gothic style, with its current majestic dimensions. The façade, currently covered for important structural repairs, is characterised by the "inflationary" use of windows with the pointed arches which we can also note in the adjacent Palazzo Giustinian. However, unlike this building, it is marked by the vertical features and above all by the large central square which encloses the two large eight-lancet

The majestic fifteenth-century façade of the palace.

UNIVERSITA DEGLI STUDI

windows of the upper floors. Continuous balconies act as the base for small marble columns of different colours with graceful capitals engraved with cactus leaves, with pointed arches topped with rosette in the first floor, and a four lancet window on the second floor. This last offers an impressive white marble engraved band representing the Foscari coat-of-arms supported by up angels carrying shields and a majestic helmet which symbolises the doge's authority of the founder of the palace.

Francesco Foscari, an expert and farsighted politician, was elected as Doge in 1423 when he was only forty-nine years old, despite extensive opposition led by his predecessor Tommaso Mocenigo. He was the youngest ever Doge and his period in office was the longest in the history of Venice, troubled by antagonism arising out of Venetian expansionism. He was also involved, although indirectly, in a scandal involving his son Jacopo.

It appears that Jacopo Foscari was to Nauplia in Rumania as a result of his accepting gifts in exchange for favours but, thanks to his father's prestige, this was converted to confinement in Treviso two years later and later cancelled. However in 1450, following the murder of the nobleman Almorò Donà, who had been a member of the Council of Ten when Jacopo was condemned to exile, Jacopo was unfairly accused and banished to the island of Crete, where he died before his innocence was recognised. His story was taken up by Byron in the tragedy I due Foscari (1821) later used by Verdi for the melodrama of the same name (1844).

Francesco Foscari died in 1457 at the age of eighty-four, three days after the Council of Ten had forced him to abdicate, because he was physically unable to fulfil his role.

In subsequent centuries, as a result of its position and the magnificence of its architecture, the palace was chosen as a residence for distinguished figures such as Ferdinand and Maximilian of Austria, Ernesto Augusto, Duke of Brunswick and King Ferninand IV of Denmark. However, the most memorable celebrations ever to be arranged by the Republic were undoubtedly those organised in 1574 to pay homage to Henry VIII of Valois, King of France and Poland. Gondolas lined with satin and damask transported the monarch and sixty senators to Murano, where they were welcomed by sixty halberdiers and forty young Venetian noblemen who were to act as his personal escort throughout his stay. On board of galley, and accompanied by the Doge, Alvise Mocenigo, the King was escorted to San Nicolò del Lido where an arch of triumph designed by Palladio and decorated by Tintoretto, Veronese and Aliene had been constructed. Finally, aboard a Bucentaur, he arrived at Palazzo Foscari, where a floating furnace had been set up, under the windows to create glass for the wonder of the King. It appears that cutlery, dishes and table decorations used for the banquet were made of sugar, according to a design by Sansovino.

During the second half of the nineteenth century the palace underwent a period of serious decline; used as an Austrian barracks, in 1844 Lecomte described it thus "on the second floor, in a remote part of the palace, today only the faithful guests of this wonderful relic remain. Their rooms are located on the right at the end of the gallery. The first room, which was once an elegant room, has been transformed into a kitchen; the tapestries, the hangings and stucco-work, everything has disappeared. The second room is in the same state, if not even worse. But who are the guests of this unfortunate hotel? They are two old septuagenarians who you can visit whenever you want: the Countesses Foscari, the last heirs of this glorious name!"

The palace was purchased by the municipality of Venice in 1847. After major restoration work the palace was used to house the University Institute of Economics and Commerce. Today it houses the main offices of the University of Venice.

Ca' Pesaro

A masterpiece of the residential architecture by Baldassarre Longhena, a magnificent representation of regal ambition, the palace seems to confirm the proud though unlikely descent of Pesaro's family from "Jupiter, King of Tuscany and Emperor of the world" (G.Zabarella). The building, which from the façade facing onto the Canal Grande extends back for almost seventy metres towards the town, stands on an extensive area purchased by the family over a period of time from 1558 until 1628, when Giovanni Pesaro began the first work. It is believed that from that time the thirty-years-old Longhena was present, in an unofficial manner, at the site which however only began serious construction work after several decades. While there is no certain documentation relating to originator of the design, Longhena's style is so evident that there is no space for attribution to others. The architect, using the consolidated base formed by pre-existent foundations, adopted a three-part design: the monumental part on the Canal Grande was distinguished by the great staircase situated in the entrance-hall, the internal courtyard with the continuous open gallery working and service areas. In 1679 the first floor was completed, but from 1682, the year of death of both Longhena and the person commissioning the work, Leonardo Pesaro (nephew of Giovanni), work halted until the beginning of the following century, when it was started once again by Antonio Gaspari, a pupil of the architect. Gaspari modified the layout, giving more importance therefore to the longitudinal features, with the elimination of the large stairway which divided the long "portego" and terminating the façade along the Canal Grande, redefining 17th century theatrical spatial quality of the courtyard and designing the façade on the Rio delle Due Torri river. The main façade, undoubtedly already concluded in 1710 according to the original project, is of exceptional

On the left: Gustav Klimt, *Giuditta II (Salomè)*, 1909.

Opposite: the façade of the palace on Canal Grande.

architectural importance, thanks to the marked play on contrast and the chiaroscuro effect, the constant exasperation of plastic details and the clash between "the geometric rationality of architecture and the manifestation of natural and fantastic principles" (G. Romanelli). On the ground floor and mezzanine floor there is a double water-gate by a vestibule, almost as if to mitigate the uniqueness nature of the central axis constituted by the entrance hall; this is characterised by the projecting diamond-shaped ashlar-work which gives it movement thanks to the full and empty spaces. The contrast with the two upper floors is very clear. These floors, which differ from each other only in terms of the continuous projecting balcony on the first floor and re-entrant on the second floor, are established within an architectural structure which emphasises the predominance of the empty rather that the full space by alternating the wide round arch windows with projecting twin columns at the corners and along the central walls. The wall surfaces on the second floor, are instead characterised by the proliferation of plastic decoration such as friezes, monsters, chimeras, scroll ornaments, putti, bearded heads and other typical marble decorations belonging to the Baroque style, which G. Romanelli compares to "the slumber of reason ready to swallow up the very

principle of rationality on which the raison d'etre of the classic architectural language was based". On the contrary the side wall by Gaspari, respecting the spirit of his maestro, offers a simpler and calmer language; the perspective made up of the series of windows which proceed towards Santa Maria Mater Domini, following the course of the canal course with a "delicate peremptory tendency" is a marvel.
The interior decoration also contributed towards asserting the grandeur of the Pesaro family.
From the solemn entrance-hall, where we find the impressive circled columns, the Roman busts and the ashlar-work together with the refinement of the pink and white striped flooring, it is possible to reach the upper floor via the monumental great staircase. Here it was once possible to admire the extensive picture-gallery of the family, which was sold by the last descendant, Pietro in 1830, and the ceiling with the oil-painting of *Zefiro and Flora* by Tiepolo, a painting currently to be found in Ca' Rezzonico. The large halls decorated with stucco-work and frescoes by Nicolò Bambini, Giambattista Pittoni and Gerolamo Brusaferro have housed the International Gallery of Modern Art in Venice since 1902, as the Duchess Felicita Bevilacqua La Masa donated the palace to the city in 1889.

The side of the palace on Rio delle Due Torri.

Ca' Rezzonico

In 1667 Filippo Bon commissioned the construction of his residence on the Canal Grande from the architect Baldassare Longhena. As Bon wanted a completely new construction and not restoration, several buildings belonging to him along the Santa Barbara river had to be demolished. Bon's idea was to create a completely new piece of art.

In 1682, before the work was completed, Longhena died and the palace had only reached the first floor. The side wings had also been finished (as documented in the prints and paintings from the era Vincenzo Coronehl), allowing Filippo Bon to live in some rooms within the building. The work was interrupted in 1750 and Bon was obliged to sell the land

and the unfinished building to the Rezzonico family. The Rezzonico family were a rich family originally from Como who had recently acquired a title (1687). They entrusted the construction of the palace to the architect Giorgio Massari. In 1752 the second floor was finished, and in 1756 the construction was completed with the

decoration of the façade, the stairway from the canal and the area to the rear, with the large atrium with its columns and the monumental and airy large staircase which led up to the huge ballroom. The intervention of Massari did not fundamentally alter Longhena's design, except for the sideways layout, as compared to the position of the 'portego', allowing the

On the left: the alcove coming from Palazzo Carminati in San Stae (second half of the Eighteenth-century).

Opposite: the façade, work of Giorgio Massari, facing on Canal Grande.

ballroom to occupy the whole width of the palace. The new hall and the grand staircase leading to it were created over the full height of two floors, thus becoming the most largest private hall within the city.

The façade is horizontally divided into three large bands: the ground floor has its ashlar-work and water gate has a three lancet entrance with architrave. On the two upper floors, the ends of which are delimited by twin columns emphasising the corners, the windows flanked by half columns are arched, with carved heads on the keystone and carved figures in the extrados. The garret is decorated with oval openings. The two upper floors have continuous balconies supported by projecting frames and barbicans.

In 1775 the family Rezzonico had gained so much power and recognition in Italy that Carlo Rezzonico was elected Pope with the name of Clemente XIII

In 1758 the wedding between Faustina Savorgnan and Ludovico Rezzonico offered the occasion to conclude the interior decoration of the palace and to take the huge building to the apex of its splendour: painters and decorators were summoned to adorn the rooms, leading to the frescoe decoration by Guarana, Gaspare Diziani and Giambattista Tiepolo.

In 1797, with the end of the Venetian Republic, the enormous quantity of objects, furniture and pictures in the palace were dispersed.

Of these original furnishings only two chandeliers, a lacquered door and the frescos have remained in the palace.

In 1810 Abbondio, the last heir of the Rezzonico family, died in Pisa. After his death the building passed to the Widmann family, and was handed down until the end of the nineteenth century, when the palace was purchased by the English painter, Robert Barret Browning.

Browning, who lived there for a long period, setting up his studio in the palace. He received the American painter John Singer Sargent as his guest in the building, together with his father Robert, who died there in 1889.

In 1935 the palace became the property of the Venetian municipality and was turned into the 18th century Venetian museum.

The huge ballroom frescoed by Giambattista Crosato. At foreground, on the right side, a sculpture in ebony of Andrea Brustolon.

Ceiling painted by Giambattista Tiepolo in 1757: *Allegory of the wedding of Lodovico Rezzonico with Faustina Savorgnan.*

Ca' Tron

The powerful and rich Venetian Tron family was of ancient origin, constituting one of the original families responsible for the construction of San Staes church in 996. From the 14th century, they lived in San Stae area in the pre-existing Byzantine Gothic construction on the Canal Grande.

The huge fortune they accumulated in the 15th century, thanks above all to trading with the East, and their strong family ties, allowed them to retain their assets, avoiding dispersion and division and overcoming increasing difficulties linked to the discovery of America and the new trading routes and allowing them to work on the complete restoration of their palace at the end of the 16th century.

The façade, with its traditional water gate and the three lancet window, displaced toward the left, recalls the influence of Sansoviani in the long modillions under the windows of the mezzanine and final floors, in the form of the balusters and in the regular columns of the four lancet windows terminating with ionic Corinthian capitals, respectively on the first and second floors and surmounted by arches. The result is a sober and luminous façade broadly praised by Francesco Sansoviano.

The interior and furnishings were also renewed and enriched, contributing towards increasing the prestige which the building and the family enjoyed, as is testified by the fact that in 1635 they were chosen by the senate to entertain a special dimplomatic mission of the King of France, Louis XIII.

In the eighteen century, according to a design by Anthony Gaspari, the architect of Palazzo Armenis, the building was further extended, constructing two wings to the internal courtyard, at the sides of the sixteenth century façade, on which there are beautiful columns with Corinthian capitals in Verona red marble, which lead to the 'portego'.

The casino (which no longer exists) was also attributed to Gaspari. Here a sumptuous and splendidly furnished ballroom was set up, with magnificent decoration painted by Louis Dorigny, to which was subsequently added ceiling decoratio, *The fall of the giants* a fresco by Jacopo Guarana, probably commissioned by Andrea Tron for the party given in honour of Emperor Joseph II in 1775.

Andrea Tron, one of the last attorneys of San Marco, was an important figure in Venetian political and cultural society, so much so that between 1750 and 1780 he gained the title of "el paron."

He was married to Caterina Dolfin, while his brother Francesco Tron was married to Cecilia Zen.

Caterina was a patron of artists and literary figures, while Cecilia was a patron of arts and sciences.

Both of them gave life to vivacious and much appreciated meetings and receptions in which culture joined with liveliness and freedom spirit.

Cecilia was also admired by her numerous guests for her beauty and her sentimental adventures, her most famous relationship being with "Count Cagliostro", this only being interrupted when this he ran away from Venice after having defrauded a merchant.

In 1800 the family Tron died out. Following the death of Cecilia, whose second marriage was to Count Giorgio Ricchi, in 1828 the building and the assets of the Tron family passed to her daughter Chiara Maria, who had married a member of the Donà delle Rose family.

Currently Palazzo Tron houses the Town Planning Department of the Architecture Faculty of the University of Venice.

The eighteenth-century frontage conceived by Antonio Gaspari.

Ca' Zenobio

Between 1690 and 1700 Antonio Gaspari built this magnificent palace close to the church of Carmini for the Zenobio family, who were rich merchants of Greek origin who had moved to Verona, Counts of the Holy Roman Empire, owners of castles and feuds in the valley of Adige and who entered the Venetian aristocracy in 1646 as a result of the payment of a considerable amount of money.

The new *status* of the family required an appropriate palace and Gaspari, who was a pupil and collaborator of Baldassarre Longhena up to that time more famous for restoration and modernisation work rather than new buildings, designed this large Baroque building, over a previously existing building dating back to the fourteenth century. The last floor of the long, austere and imposing façade is decorated with an enormous curved tympanum in roman style (indeed Gaspari was probably the only Venetian architect of the period to be influenced by the decorative and structural language of Bernini and Borromini) and on the first floor with a large three mullioned window with

a continuous projecting balcony. In truth the façade hides a complex C-shaped plan, opening out to the rear onto a large Italian style garden. At the bottom of this garden at the end of the eighteenth century, Tomaso Temanza built a pavilion already adopting neo-classical features, used as a library and archive.

Inside, the large and luxurious ballroom situated on the main floor is decorated with white and gold stucco-work and it is separated from the short gallery by a large three-mullioned central arch window which supports a curved music gallery with elaborate corbels. Enormous mirrors are mounted on the walls, increasing the space and light. The most brilliant artists in Venice in the period were recruited to decorate

Above: the frontage of the palace on Canal Carmini.

Opposite: the ballrooom frescoed by Louis Dorigny and Antonio Gaspari.

The hall on the noble floor with Luca Carlevarijs paintings.

the palace. Louis Dorigny painted the famous ceiling of the large ballroom with a glorification of the Zenobio family; Luca Carlevarijs – so linked to the family that he was known as Luca from Ca' Zenobio – painted the three landscapes situated in the portico; Gianbattista Tiepolo painted the fresco on the ceiling, which has unfortunately been transferred elsewhere; Abbondio Stazio was probably responsible for the magnificent and complex stucco decoration.

After the death of the last male heir, the palace was inherited by Alba Zenobio Albrizzi and the rich library and the art collection was moved to Palazzo Albrizzi, in Venice.

At present Ca' Zanobio houses the Armenian Mekhitarist College.

Casa Torres

Access to the small building is gained from the Gaffaro foundations along the canal of the same name, a broad service canal which leads from Malcanton towards Piazzale Roma. The building is a characteristic "artist's house" built between 1905 and 1907 by the Venetian architect Giuseppe Torres for himself and his family, and is probably the clearest demonstration of the new medieval architectural style in the city. The building recalls a medieval house with underlying workshop in the Venetian-Byzantine style of the façade, the mullioned-window on the first floor and the corner windows. An important example of such a house is situated in the nearby Campo Santa Margherita. The façade is decorated with fresco paintings with tiny neo-medieval motifs and topped upside-down truncated cone chimneys which recall the paintings of Vittore Carpaccio, giving to the building a fantastic and magical quality, both intimate and distant. Other distinctive features of the villa and the architect (another work by him is the restoration and renovation of Ca' Barzizza and San Silvestro, not far from Rialto) are the picturesque play on volume, the choice of materials and the colours, both outside and inside. Casa Torres has also, a small, but very suggestive garden in a private courtyard which gives it a more "romantic" appearance.

The eclectic façade of Casa Torres on Gaffaro foundations along the Canal Grande of the same name.

Fondaco dei Turchi

Considered to be the most significant Venetian – Byzantine residential building in Venice, Fondaco dei Turchi "was one of the most important palaces on the Canal Grande, and (...) when it was handed over to the restorers, it resembled an imposing ruin, looking at which the regret felt for everything the building had lost over the centuries was mitigated by admiration for what remained of the precious material and of the even more precious sculptures". This is how Boni described the state of the building at the end of 19th century, before radical restoration which finished in 1869 according to a project by Federico Berchet, which involved the substitution of the original building with what Concina describes as an "extremely Venetian reinvention of image (...) and model (...) both in terms of fifty years of restoration (...) and of the tenacious recovery of the Byzantine style, and finally of the rapid diffusion of paterae, panels, reused cornices and (...) imitation of thousands of false sculptures in the architectural decoration".
The original project is

reintroduced with a façade framed between two side towers, which constitutes a typical feature of many palaces in the period, while the main floor has wide windows and a portico offering access to the canal, the largest one existing in Venice after the later example of the Palazzo Ducale, designed for the loading and unloading of merchandise from boats coming from East and West. The palace was commissioned by the rich merchant Giacomo Calmieri of Pesaro, probably in the first decades of thirteenth century, and in 1381 it had already been bought by the Venetian Republic, against the will of Angelo Pesaro who had forbidden his heirs to sell the palace, in order to give it as a gift to Nicolò d'Este, Marquis of Ferrara, as recognition for his loyalty during the war of Chioggia. From that time the palace was repeatedly granted and confiscated by Venice to the Estensi family as a result of

The façade rebuilt in the nineteenth century by Federico Berchet.

their political U-turns, as took place from 1509 to 1527, when the Lords of Ferrara joined the anti-Venetian league of Cambrai. The palace was often used by the Republic to provide hospitality to distinguished figures, such as Giovanni VIII Paleologo, Emperor of Byzantium, accompanied by almost six hundred and fifty orthodox priests.

Finally in 1602 it was handed over to the Cardinal Aldobrandini who sold it to Antonio Priuli in 1618, when he was elected Doge.

The advisability of giving a specific office to Turkish merchants had been discussed for many years. The idea, which had grown out of the need to avoid incidents which could have ruined diplomatic relations between Venice and the Sultan, was only fulfilled in 1621 when the work to adapt the interior started, in order to transform it into a new warehouse for the Turks, where twenty-four storerooms, fifty-two rooms, wash-houses, services and a mosque had been created. Nevertheless prejudice and provisions against the Turks continued, as testified by the fact that young men and Christian women were forbidden access.

When, after the Candia war, trade began to decline, the number of merchants also diminished, thus leading to slow and continuous decline that ended with the partial collapse in 1732. The palace again became the property of the Pesaro family and then passed to the Manin family. In 1838, when the last Turkish merchant was expelled, a certain Saddo-Drisdi, the building was in a state of serious decay. It was therefore bought, for the sum of eight thousand florins, by the Municipality in 1860, who after the aforementioned restoration used it as a museum. At present it houses the Museum of Natural History.

Opposite: one of the Museum of Natural History rooms.

Above: the warehouse before the restorations in the nineteenth-century.

Palazzo Albrizzi

The façade on Rio di San Cassiano.

The Albrizzi family arrived in Venice from Bergamo during the 16th century. They had a considerable fortune thanks to the commerce of cloth and oil and had rendered themselves useful to the country by offering their merchant ships for the war of Candia against the Turks. This, together with the payment of one hundred thousand ducats to the Treasury, contributed to the admission of Antonio Albrizzi's sons to the Higher Council on 31 May 1667. On his death, Giuseppe, Giovanni Battista, Alessandro and Anton Francesco Albrizzi also inherited Palazzo Bonomo on the canal of S. Cassiano, acquired between 1648 and 1692. The new palazzo Albrizzi, is majestic and solemn; the façade overlooking the canal centred on the three-mullioned central arched window, flanked by pairs of single lancet windows with projecting stone cornices which act as a small roof. This is interrupted, such well-defined sections of wall that it has been suggested that there was pictorial decoration. The somewhat dreary of the exterior contrasts with the wealth of the interior which reflects well the patronage of the family.

Between 1690 and 1710 the interior space was totally redefined, with an excessive use of decoration and stucco-work, which makes the palace one of the most ostentatious in Venice. Under the direction of artists such as Antonio Gaspari, Abbondio Stazio and Carpoforo Mazzetti, known as Tencalla, the high-relief stucco decoration in lively colours extended over large areas, becoming the true protagonist of the space. It is impossible not to be impressed by the square ballroom "covered" with the elegant draped pavilion and supported by twenty-eight small angels in flight and the marvellous ceiling of the portico where putti hiding behind the curtains bearing aristocratic coats-of-arms combine with mythological

The majestic "pórtego" decorated with stuccoes of Abbondio Stazio.

subjects and cornices which hold paintings of the Albrizzi family. In these rooms, Isabella Teotochi, wife of Giuseppe Albrizzi, established a literary drawing-room visited by figures such as Ippolito Piedemonte, Vincenzo Monti, Lord Byron, Vittorio Alfieri and Ugo Foscolo; this last is known to have had a relationship with her extending beyond friendship. The sculptor Antonio Canova also participated in the society life of the palace and he gave a *Head of Helen* to the lady of the house.

In 1771 the Albrizzi family had some buildings demolished in order to enlarge the factory and to obtain sufficient to give suitable prominence to the façade. It is interesting to remember that the Nuovo Teatro di San Cassian, which was one of the first public theatres for comedies in Venice and in the whole of Europe, was situated near the palace. It was demolished in 1812, leaving more space for the gardens of the palace, which is still inhabited by the descendants of the old owners.

Palazzo Ariani

The origin of the Ariani family is unclear: according to some they were from Istria, according to other from Capitanata. However by the 9th century they were already the owners of a large part of the area surrounding the current church of the Angelo Raffaele.

Due to an accusation of fraudulent bankruptcy around the middle of the 14th century, the Ariani family was deprived of its noble title. The head of family Antonio so deeply resented this that he ordered in his will that none of his descendants should marry members of the Venetian aristocracy, subject to loss of their inheritance. In any event the Ariani family tried unceasingly to recover their title by offering large sums of money to the Treasury, without reaching any positive result; apparently on the umpteenth refusal Marco Ariani decided to become a monk in Ferrara.

Palazzo Ariani lies at the meeting of the San Basegio, Carmini and Angelo Raffaele canals. The current palace was reconstructed during the second half of 14th century and is unique in terms of its style. The wonderful six-mullioned window, perfectly framed by the indented frieze, is not linked to any architectural sequence; while the section made up of three columns and two pillars and the parapets are part of the Venetian tradition, the innovation lies in the filling of the upper band above the windows. The double row of quatrefoil windows defined by a torus moulding, which results in the "soft profile" of French influence, and the hive-shaped openwork, reminiscent of English models though less elaborate, appear for the first time in this Gothic Venetian building, anticipating the arches of the Palazzo Ducale. Another uncommon feature is the wooden architrave which characterised corner, creating a lower portico held up by columns which look out over the courtyard from which the external two-flight staircase departs. The architectural organisation and the solutions adopted give a " rudimentary" aesthetic impression and consequently the design can be attributed to a stone-worker-architect coming from outside the environment.

The palace remained the property of the Ariani family until 1650 when the last descendant, Giacomo, left it to the Patrice family from Pasqualigo. In the second half of the eighteenth century it became the property of the brothers Antonio and Carlo Pasinetti, while one floor was rented to a lady from the Cicogna family, once a Benedictine nun, who established girls' college there. In 1849 it was bought by the Municipality of Venice, who used it as a primary school, a use which still continues.

The gothic façade on Rio dell'Angelo Raffaele.

Palazzo Balbi

Tassini narrates an amusing anecdote as regards the origin of this palace: "A certain gentleman (N. Balbi) was living not far from there, in a rented house, but quite innocently he forgot to pay the rent by the deadline, so one day on his way to the Higher Council, he was accosted by the owner of the house who bluntly invited him to pay up. Nicolò paid, but immediately terminated the agreement, giving orders to initiate the construction of a palace. In the meantime, together with his family, he moved into a large ship moored on the banks of the canal, obscuring the view of the house inhabited by which the man who had so rudely approached him in the street".

Built in only eight years (1582-1590) according to a design by Alessandro Vittoria, Palazzo Balbi dominates "the bend in the Canal" between the Accademia and the Ponte di Rialto, in a picturesque position which inspired artists such as Canaletto and Marieschi.

The building has an important role in the history of Venetian architecture; indeed while the layout and the division of the façade into three is not unusual, analysis of the individual architectural features demonstrates the passage from the highlight of classicism to the early Baroque era. Vittoria, who was a pupil of Sansovino, made use of architectural and decorative elements such as the central mullioned-window balustrade, the mixtilinear tympanums, the sinuous frames of the windows and the two coats-of-arms carved in high relief with scroll volutes within a space organised according to the classical arrangement of pillars, giving all the features an innovative plastic quality thanks to the play on light and shade resulting from the greater or lesser accentuation of the objects.

The magnificence of the palace, which gives the lie to an old proverb which states that "among things which cannot be found in Venice there are rich members of the Balbi family", was imitated in the city for a long time and matches the imposing Ca' Foscari as a background to the "machina", the platform of arrival for rowing competitions during historic regattas. In 1807 Napoleon watched a regatta organised in his honour from a special loggia set up along its façade. The palace was sold to the antique dealer Michelangelo Guggenheim in 1887 and was subsequently purchased by the Adriatica Electrical Company in 1925. It was fully restored in 1973 and since then has been the seat of the regional council for the Veneto region.

Palazzo Balbi dominates "the bend in the Canal" in a picturesque position.

Palazzo Barbaro

Of the two adjacent palaces, one of which is gothic and the other in Baroque style, which make up Palazzo Barbaro complex, one was designed by Giovanni Bon in 1425, while the second was designed by Antonio Gaspari, a pupil of Longhena, around 1694. The Barbaro family, one of the most famous houses, whose name would appear derive from the action of a certain Marco who in 1121 retrieved the flag of San Marco from the barbarians, while he was in the army led by Doge Domenico Michiel in the Holy Land, was already present in the city in 869 after having moved from Roma to Istria, then to Trieste and finally to Venice. Originally the gothic palace was owned by the Spiera family, then it was purchased by Zaccaria Barbaro in the fifteenth century. The façade has the traditional three-part arrangement, archaic features mixing together with decidedly fifteenth century components: on the first floor the mullioned-window with quatrefoil work stands out, while on the second floor the windows, which recall the fourteenth century style due to their height, are finished with curved arches on tall columns terminating with capitals with leaf motifs. The two water gates cannot pass unnoticed: the original portal with curved arch formed the head of a gallery facing on to the Canal Grande, now blocked, along the side of the Rio Orso canal, whereas the renaissance gate is evidence of one of the many architectural interventions carried out during the centuries.

The building designed by Gaspari by the end of the seventeenth century reflects with sober grandeur not only the social position of the family, but also the established role of members of the family within the literary and artistic scene. Daniele and Marc'Antonio had already shown themselves to be men of culture and enlightened patrons commissioning the construction of Villa Maser according to a design by Palladio with frescoes by Veronese. They were the great grandsons of Ermolao "Armerò" Barbaro, who in 1491 was chosen by the Pope to be patriarch of Aquileia, causing moral indignation in the Venetian Republic. Daniele and Marc'Antonio supported the design of Palladio for the construction of Ponte di Rialto; they also rescued Paolo Veronese, who was accused of irreverence for painting a *Last Supper* which was considered too worldly, coming up with the idea of changing the name of the painting to *Dinner at the Levi House*. Behind a long, narrow façade marked by two lancet windows and single light pointed arch windows, of which those on the main floor were taller, the interiors are surprising for the richness of the furnishings. The ballroom, an excellent example of local Baroque style, is till today embellished with stucco decoration, within which there are paintings by Sebastiano Ricci and G.B. Piazzetta, while the paintings realised by Giambattista Tiepolo are at present held at the Metropolitan Museum in New York. The elegant eighteenth century library situated on the third floor, with lowered ceiling is a riot of multicoloured stucco decoration, with innocent Cupids surrounding the golden stucco medallions, the walls marked alternately by open bookcases and large windows stretching up from the floor.

When the Republic fell and the family died out, the palace was purchased a married couple called Curtis. They were Americans from Boston, art-lovers and they opened up the house to personages such as Robert Browning, J.S. Sargent, Claude Monet and the writer Henry James, who wrote the Aspern correspondence here, describing the magnificent rooms of the palace in his novel *The Wings of the Dove*. The upper floors of the seventeenth century palace are still inhabited by the descendants of the Curtis family.

The façades of Palazzo Barbaro.

Palazzo Belloni Battagia

Above: the façade of the palace; on the right a foreshortening of Fondaco del Megio.

Opposite: the entrance hall on the noble floor.

In 1647 the Belloni family became part of the Venetian aristocracy and bought a palace on the Canal Grande. Without doubt Bortolo Belloni ordered its restoration, probably from Longhena who during the same period was finishing the plans for Palazzo Pesaro. The architectural features of the façade, as well as the accuracy and elegance of the working would appear to confirm the hand of the architect: the interrupted tympanums placed at the top of the doors and windows on the main floor, characterised by the extended modules recalling the pre-existing fourteenth building are unmistakable. The dignity of the façade resulting from the stone surfaces is almost compromised by the wit of the details: the lions heads at water level which seem to carry the whole building on their backs and the fabulous heads on the keystone, the two magnificent coats-of-arms on the main floor, the unusual masks on the two pinnacles and the frieze where crescent moons and the stars on the owner's coat-of-arms alternate. They invested almost all the fortune they had earned by practising as lawyers and in the commerce, in order to finish the palace. In 1663 it was apparently rented to Count Czernin, the Ambassador of Austria. It then became the property of the Battagia family – who apparently obtained their Venetian aristocratic title by ceding the fortress of Cremona to the Republic – and in 1804 it was purchased by the merchant Antonio Capovilla. He was responsible for the major intervention in terms of internal modernisation which cost the huge amount of one hundred thousand ducats.

Detail of Giambattista Canal frescoes.

Every reference to the homogeneity of the seventeenth century façade was cancelled; the length of the portico, the large hall of the main floor was reduced and lowered ceilings reduced the excessive height of the rooms.

Giambattista Canal, known as "the last of the quick Tiepolos" and David Rossi were instructed to deal with the interior decoration, which was then clearly influenced by Venetian neo-classicism.

What was once the central hall was divided in two. Access to the hall, overlooking the Canal Grande, with its decoration full of references to Anglo-French style in tones of white and powder blue, was gained via an entrance hall which became a genuine optical illusion, thanks to open galleries with perspective colonnades with scenes from the Homeric world.

The main floor is today the property of Institute of Foreign Commerce, whereas the rest of the palace is used as a private residence.

Palazzo Bembo

The Bembo family, originally from Bologna, was among the most ancient families in Venice: in 697 they participate in the election of the first Doge of the Venetian Republic. The palace was a mighty Gothic construction overlooking the banks of the Riva del Carbon and with the San Salvador canal on the other side.

However, Pietro Bembo does not seem to have belonged to this branch of the family. He was a Cardinal and was born in Venice in 1479. An erudite figure of the era, he was the secretary of Pope Leo X and a friend of Lucrezia Borgia and Caterina Corner.

The current building is the result of total reconstruction during the 15th century (incorporating the pre-existing 11th century Byzantine building, recognisable in the elaborate cornice of inverted acanthus leaves, inserted as a string course under the first upper floor) and of modifications carried out in the 17th century.

The façade, closed by spiral columns and quoins, is wider than it is tall, following a specular symmetrical arrangement on the vertical median axis, which seems to carry the two central five lancet windows, united only subsequently by a continuous balcony, evidence of the joining of two aristocratic houses.

As compared for example to the somewhat uncertain organisation of the Giustinian complex, Palazzo Bembo is perhaps one of the more successful examples of combined houses along the Canal Grande.

The frontage of the palace.

Palazzo Bernardo

The two water gates and the two main floors, one of which is less important than the other, of the homogeneous and grandiose façade of Palazzo Bernardo at San Polo along the Canal Grande, are an indication that interior is actually divided into two dwellings. The palace was built around in 1442, initially it would appear for two families belonging to the Bernardo house. Subsequently the building took on a public function, offering hospitality to important figures visiting Venice, such as Duke Francesco Sforza with his wife Bianca Visconti at the end of 15th century, while the owners withdrew to the other half of the building. This requirement thus explains the presence not only of the two water gates and the two main floors, but also the two land gates, the two courtyards and the two staircases.
"An important page in architecture (…) with the nonchalant and imaginative grandeur which emanates, somewhat intolerant to predetermined patterns" (E. Arslan), the façade is framed with vertical bands of hewn stones alternating with small spiral columns and dominated by the big six-mullioned window on the second floor, which recalls in a surprising manner the trefoil arch motif of the gallery of the Doge's Palace, flanked by single light windows with interesting openwork and intertwined arches. However the shifting of the simpler six-mullioned window on the first floor with the consequential moving of the right-hand water gate as compared to the distribution of the façade, strictly symmetrical in relation to the central vertical axis.

The frontage on Canal Grande.

Palazzo dei Camerlenghi

Palazzo Camerlenghi was one of the first buildings in Europe to be exclusively dedicated to offices and it takes its name from one of the financial and judicial offices which once occupied it, the Camerlenghi of Comun. Today it still has a similar function (it is indeed the seat of the accounting courts). The building is one of the few palaces in Venice to be free on all the sides and lies opposite the Ponte di Rialto in the financial centre of the city. The building as it exists today was realised by Scarpagnino between 1525 and 1528, under the dogate of Andrea Gritti, as indicated on the stone on the façade overlooking the bridge, and was the last of several architectural modifications made to emphasise the representative role of the palace: "the treasure chest of the State's, through the rich marble cladding, and the rigour of the Republic (…) through the display of the culprits, each accessible and visible from the outside" (Calabi-Moracchiello). Deprived of a genuine façade and "completely surrounded by diamond-shaped stones" (Sanudo), the palace is characterised by the white marble façades, clearly influenced by Renaissance style.

The uniformity of the cladding is marked by pilasters and entableture on which the windows with columns and round arches rest; the only decorative concessions are the frieze, carefully carved with garlands, and the medallions, once also embellished with porphyry and multicoloured marble.

The capitals placed at the sides of entrance portals representing a man with a large paw with claws between his legs and a seated woman with her vagina in flames are undoubtedly an ornamental licence. Tradition has it that these images came from a couple of common people, a man and a woman, who were involved in an animated discussion in a tavern as regards the slowness of the construction of the Ponte di Rialto – the bridge had indeed burnt down in 1514 and was only completed in 1587– apparently declared respectively: "it will be finished when my penis comes up with claws" and "when my vagina catches fire".

Inside all the paintings have been removed: the tradition which established that each magistrate should leave a painting with their portrait or coat-of-arms at the end of their period of office had created a substantial collection.

When in 1806 Venice was admitted to the Kingdom of Italy the paintings were lost: among these works by Bonifacio de' Pitati, today kept at the Galleries of the Accademia and the Cini Foundation.

The palace lapped by the high water.

Palazzo Centani

This originally belonged to the Rizzo family, whose coat-of-arms representing a hedgehog can be recognised on the marvellous 15th century well-curb in the internal courtyard. For many years the building was rented to the Centani family, taking their name. In 1537 it appears to have been inhabited by Marco, the son of Antonio Centani who was captured by Turks and sawn alive between two planks in 1500.

Carlo Goldoni was born in this house. It was the Venetian playwright who recognised it as his home in his autobiography: " I was born in Venice, in 1707, in a big beautiful house between the Nombili bridge and Donna Onesta bridge, at the corner of Calle di Ca' Centani, in the San Tomà parish".

Recent and radical restoration work has allowed the original gothic building to be recovered. It is typical of Venetian residential architecture at the end of the 14th century and in the 15th century. The façade, with uncovered brickwork, bends in order to follow the course of the canal and centres on the four-lancet window with extended columns and round arches, flanked by single light windows framed by dentate surround. Entry is through the typical internal courtyard with the uncovered two-flight staircase on pointed arches and baluster in Istria stone with cylindrical pillars, small lion and crowns.

At the beginning of the twentieth century the palace, whose decline over time had become worrying, became the object of interest by scholars of Goldoni's studious and was subsequently bought by a committee of private citizens in 1914. In 1931 the building was donated to the Municipality of Venice, which on 4 June 1953 inaugurated "Goldoni's House" which contains an extensive library of theatre texts and the International Institute for Theatrical Research.

Above: façade on Rio di San Tomà.

Opposite: the uncovered staircase inside the courtyard.

Palazzo Coccina Tiepolo Papadopoli

The palace was commissioned in the middle of the sixteenth century by a family from Bergamo called Coccina from the architect Gian Giacomo dei Grigi. This attribution has been object of some perplexity as a result of the presence of architectural features which recall well-known architecture from the sixteenth century. Indeed, on the well-proportioned and classical façade, which is completely covered with Istria stone, we find the central three lancet windows of Sanmicheli, the side windows with triangular curved tympanum reminiscent of Palladio and the oval windows with cartouche frames typical of Sansovino and Vittoria. The Coccina family, who were major collectors, here gathered together important works of art such as four paintings by Veronese, among which there is also *The family Coccina in front of the Virgin*, where we can recognise the palace, sold in 1645 to the Estensi family and at present held at the Gemäldgalerie in Dresden and *The Charlatan* and *The Minuet* by Gian Domenico Tiepolo, at present in the Museum of Barcelona. When the family died out in 1748 the palace was purchased by the Tiepolo family subsequently in 1837 by Valentino Pomello. Maddalena Montalban, the wife of Valentino Pomello, was known for her anti-Austrian political commitment, which also led to her spending a year in prison. After other transfers of the property the palace was purchased in 1864 by Counts Aldobrandini-Papadopoli, who instructed the architect Gerolamo Levi to carry out major restoration work which, together with the decoration carried out by the antiquarian Michelangelo Guggenheim, fundamentally modified the interior. The exterior was also modified; the side garden developed following the demolition of some small houses standing beside the palace.
Since 1922 the Arrivabene family have been the owners of the palace.

The white frontage of the middle sixteenth-century on Canal Grande.

Palazzo Contarini del Bovolo

A 15th century late Gothic palace, with its façade looking out over the San Luca canal, it is only partly visible from the Verona bridge. It is characterised by three five-mullioned windows placed upon above the other with gothic arches and contained within cornices with string-courses and by two water gates. It takes its name from the spiral staircase, called *bovolo* in Venetian dialect at the rear. This staircase, commissioned from the architect Giovanni Candi around 1499 by the senators Marco, Nicolò and Giovanni Battista Contarini, has since become such a characteristic feature that it led to the renaming not only of the palace but also of the Contarini family.

The helicoidal stairway, not uncommon in Venetian gothic style, develops within a tower marked by round rampant arches, finishing with a belvedere surmounted by a dome which is linked to the open gallery on five floors, one above the other. What is astoundng is not so much the less than perfect realisation undoubtedly the result of "the decisive but rough hand of a beginner" but its dimensions: the overall effect is indeed emphasised by the out-of-scale architectural elements "so it appears to be an over enlarged photo of a smaller project" (H. McAndrew).

In 1717 Elisabetta Contarini married Giovanni Minelli, a trader from Bergamo, who had joined the aristocracy through the patment of one hundred thousand ducats, bring the palace with her as her dowry. In 1803 it was sold to Arnoldo Marseille who transformed it into a hotel called "the Maltese Hotel". Today it is the seat of a charitable organisation.

On the left: the back of the palace characterised by the staircase enclosed in the tower.

Opposite: the development of the staircase from which arises the name of "bovolo".

Palazzo Contarini delle Figure

Palazzo Contarini delle Figure takes its name from the two figures under the principal balcony, which common people have interpreted as a man tears his hair out because he has lost everything gambling and his angry wife. The palace was rebuilt between 1504 and 1546 according to a design by Antonio Abbondi, known as Scarpagnino.

The perfect vertical and horizontal three-part arrangement of the façade organises architectural features of the period with details and decorations which appear to result from a more mature culture; the triangular tympanum is indeed particularly unexpected, being a feature only taken up in the eighteenth century by pre neo-classicists, which highlights the Corinthian four-mullioned window with channelled columns. The naturalistic character of the delicate decoration, described by Ruskin as an "image of the dying naturalism of gothic art" also seems to reflect the cultural and artistic eclecticism of the commissioners, making this palace an example of renaissance architecture with the most refined façade along the Canal Grande.

The richness and the attention to detail, the capitals of the façade probably painted in gold, and the countless works of art in the interior link Jacopo Contarini to this building without a doubt. An attorney of the Venetian Republic, which assigned him with the task of reorganising the program for the painting of the hall of the Higher Council and within the Palace Ducale, he was described as follows by Girolamo Porro:

"a connoisseur of all beautiful things, whether architecture, picture, sculpture or weapons

On the left: one of the coat of arms which decorates the renaissance façade.

Opposite: the façade with the unusual central tympanum

and musical instruments ...., almost a new Archimedes.... with excellent judgement in all the sciences and arts". He collected works of art by Bassano, Tiziano, Tintoretto, Palma the Younger, scientific volumes and architectural drawings; among these there were the drawings he received as a present from his friend Andrea Palladio, who lived there in 1570, which are currently conserved in the Royal Institute of British Architects in London.

In 1713 according to the will of Bertucci, the last of the Contarini family, all the furniture and the works of art, among which the magnificent *Ratto d'Europa* by Veronese, became part of the collection of the Doge's Palace. In the 19th century the palace was purchased by the Marquises Guiccioli; the wife of Alessandro Guiccioli, Teresa, is recalled as the last great love of Lord Byron, who rented the neighbouring palace for a long time.

At present the building is privately owned and has been divided into several apartments.

Opposite: the large hall on the noble floor.

On the right: the monumental chimney surmounted by stuccoes figures and the frieze with golden frames which enclose mythological scenes.

Palazzo Contarini Fasan

Palazzo Contarini Fasan, thus called due to the presumed passion of one of its owners for the hunting of pheasants, represents a unique example of late gothic Venetian architecture at the end of the 15ᵗʰ century. It was probably constructed between 1470 and 1480; its small façade is confined between denticulate corner bands with Istria stone quoins alongside small spiral columns and displays balance in terms of its proportions and symmetry. The richness of the architectural elements and the florid gothic decoration without Renaissance details bring the palace, as also noted by Ruskin, closer to northern taste typical of English and French gothic architecture. The marble capitals and the balconies decorated with round wheel openwork are interesting for their sober richness and the prestigious fret work, also reintroduced in the three-mullioned window of the large hall and in the two single light windows, creating a lively and intense decorative uniformity.

Popular tradition has it that this was the house of Desdemona, who was the wife and victim of the jealousy of the Moor Othello, immortalised in Shakespeare's tragedy.

Below: detail of the marble balcony enriched with the theme of wheel-engraved.

Opposite: the narrow late-gothic façade.

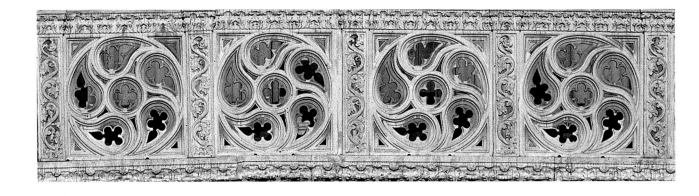

Palazzo Contarini Dal Zaffo

"Severe but decorated with sculptures which are unrivalled for their audacity of touch and for the careful grace of shape.... for the use of coloured marble, serpentines and porphyries" (Ruskin), the façade blends Byzantine forms with classic-antique elements, neglecting the traditional gothic repertory, in an unusual manner for this era.

The palace that was built at the end of 15th century and was purchased in the middle of the 16th century by one of the oldest Venetian families, the Contarini family – from the city of Jaffa in the East – which origined in *gens romana* Aurelia Cotta, a relative of Caesar's mother, who participated at the election of the first Doge in 697.

The architect, presumably Mauro Condussi or Pietro Lombardo, introduced a new antique decoration culture of Tuscan influence with balanced proportions, respecting the three-part arrangement of the façade framed in "ancient style" by parastades and trabeations. The central five-mullioned window and the long windows with archivolts are embellished with low-relief, marble cladding, polychrome tondi and large clypeus in precious marble, in a compositional style which is so light that it makes the building, which is not impressive in terms of size, an example of refinement and elegance. In the 18th century Giandomenico Tiepolo decorated the interior with rich decoration, among which there is a frieze representing Satyrs, vases, musical instruments and Roman triumphs, together with a painting, which was exported to Cologne and was unfortunately destroyed.

In 1758 the palace was sold by Alvise Contarini of Giorgio to the Manzoni family, originally from Bergamo, who made thir fortune through the commerce of silk. It was subsequently purchased by the Polignac-Decazes Dukes, who are still the owners. In the first decades of the 20th century, Princess Polignac received famous figures from the artistic world here, competing with the most famous salons of the period.

The marble decorated façade refined (end of fifteenth century).

Palazzo Corner della Ca' Granda

Palazzo Corner della Ca' Granda "...dares to break the continuity of Canal Grande with its dimensions and its triumphal language" (M. Tafuri).

The ashlar base, the volute corbels, the façade marked by a parade of classical features which by then only hinted at central tripartite arrangement, the oval windows with cartouche cornices and the internal open courtyard in the Roman manner reveal a formal language of central Italy which isolates the architecture from the context, transforming itself into a proud instrument celebrating the person commissioning the palace.

It lies on the site of the pre-existing Palazzo Malombra, destroyed by a fire in 1532, which Giorgio Corner, brother of the Queen of Cyprus, had bought at the height of his economical, political and social life. It would appear that the fire was caused by the drying of a stock of sugar, coming from the sugar cane plantations in the Cypriot feud of Piscopia. The palace on Canal Grande housed not only residential accommodation and offices but was also a warehouse and working area; the coal fires lit for the drying process led to a disaster which Marin Sanudo, who was an eye witness, describes thus in the *Diari* "nothing remained, only the bank with the columns, the rest was burned and destroyed". Its reconstruction was assigned to Jacopo Sansovino, who had arrived from Rome at the end of 1527, by the nephew of Giorgio Corner, Zorzetto, who was loyal to the proudly papal line followed by the family. Work started in 1533 and ended after 1556, apparently under the direction of Scamozzi.

On 13 February 1812 Alvise Corner sold the palace to the State; the interior was emptied and the furniture and paintings, including paintings by Tintoretto, Raffaello, Tiziano and Palma the Older, were dispersed. The well-curb, perhaps by Sansovino, since 1824 has been held at Campo Santo Giovanni e Paolo. Again in this period the floor of the internal courtyard, on which Fontana recalls a "the tracing in bright red stone of a sort of maze which had been created for the entertainment of the family (...)" was replaced with the current stone flagging.

In 1814 the palace became the office of the Provincial Austrian Delegation and following the unification of Italy, it became office of the Prefecture.

The majestic façade in Sansovino's style on Canal Grande.

Palazzo Corner Loredan Piscopia

The palace, while representing a modification of the sixteenth century building, still followed the pattern of the Venetian Byzantine house-storehouse. Architectural and decorative elements such as the five-arch loggia directly over the water and, on the main floor, the "façade completely covered by the many lancet window" (S. Bettini) with round arches on pilasters and capitals resting on fine twin columns in line with the interior division of the rooms mean that the architecture is undoubtedly inspired by the thirteenth century model. From the beginning the palace belonged to a family from Parma called Boccasi. It then passed to the Zane family, which in 1361 acted as host to the court of the Duke of Austria, and finally to one of the most important Venetian families: the Corners. The chronicles of the era report says that in 1363 Pietro II of Lusignano, King of Cyprus, threatened by the Turks, was received by Federico Corner as a guest and treated in a princely manner. In order to thank him for the concession of a large loan, the King assigned the feud of Piscopia to Federico Corner with right to cultivate and refine sugar free of fiscal and customs duties, and appointed him as Knight of the Order of the Sword. On the façade of the palace there was heraldic-allegorical decoration representing David and Goliath, on the right and left respectively, while in the middle there was the symbol of the knighthood of the Order of the Sword between a depiction of Justice and Force.

Valentina Visconti, the promised bride of King Pietro II, also lived in the palace in 1377, while in 1389 Francesco Gonzaga, Lord of Mantua lived there.

In the 17th century the palace was restored by the penultimate heir of the Corners, Giovanni Battista, attorney of San Marco. His marriage to Zanetta Bonis, who came from a very modest family, made such a sensation that the Avogaria of Comun, the custodian of "Golden Book", did not recognise the marriage with the consequential exclusion of male children from the Higher Council. It took a payment of approximately one hundred and five thousand ducats and four petitions to obtain the right in 1664 for their sons, Francesco and Girolamo to be admitted to the Venetian aristocracy. However if the marriage upset high society, their daughter, Elena Lucrezia was a very important figure in terms of female emancipation in a cultural environment. She was born in 1646, and was immediately entrusted to the tutoring of a cultured priest and subsequently to Alvise Ambrogio Gradenigo, an erudite librarian of the Marciana. After having studied Latin, Greek, Hebrew, French, Spanish, Mathematics, sacred history and music and having followed dialectical and philosophy courses at Padua university, she was denied a degree in theology, obtaining instead a degree in philosophy, awarded on 25 June 1678. Suffering from poor health, she dedicated herself to asceticism and died at the age of only thirty-eight in her family's palace in Padua.

In 1703 the palace became property of the Loredan family after the marriage between one of Girolamo Corner's daughters with Giovanni Battista Loredan. In 1806 Lucrezia Maria, the daughter of Cristoforo Loredan, sold the palace. It was transformed into a hotel after having been purchased and restored by Countess Campagna Peccana and was finally acquired by the municipal government of Venice in 1867. It currently houses the town hall.

The façade on Canal Grande.

Palazzo Corner-Mocenigo

On the area overlooking the canal of San Paolo, where at present there is Palazzo Corner-Mocenigo, there was once a fourteenth century building, called the "Palace of the Cagnon", given as a present by the Republic to Francesco Sforza, who exchanged it with a property in San Samuele belonging to the Corner family around 1460. The fourteenth century palace was completely destroyed by a fire in 1535, and Giovanni Corner, nephew of the King of Cyprus, ordered its reconstruction from the architect of the Republic, Michele Sanmicheli. In 1564, four years after his death, the building was finished. Palazzo Corner-Mocenigo was undoubtedly admired for its six floors, which were very unusual for the period; it was described by Vasari as "magnificent and majestic rich" and by Sansovino as "with a wealth of rich decorations".

The façade is characterised by stumpy pillars and by the two large central three-lancet windows with non-projecting balconies which subordinate practicality aesthetic requirements. The frugal decorative elements and the limited use of marbles and Istria stone suggest a prototype realisation for a more important customer. On the canal the three arched portals demonstrate the original intention of building the palace for three different families, ensuring complete independence for the entrances; indeed the sons of Giovanni Corner occupied only the main floor and rented the others. In 1799 the last descendant of this branch of the Corner family, Giovanni, donated the palace to his daughter as a dowry on her marriage to Alvise Mocenigo, who thus became the owner. The building currently houses the headquarters of Customs Officers.

On the left: the façade on Rio di San Polo.

Opposite: the side of the palace towards Campo San Polo.

Palazzo Corner Spinelli

Palazzo Corner-Spinelli was commissioned by the Lando family in 1480-90, and in 1542 was sold by Pietro Lando di Marco, Archbishop of Candia, to Giovanni Corner. It was purchased after the fire which destroyed Palazzo Corner in San Polo in 1535, Giovanni decided to modify the interior to his own needs, with the assistance of Sanmicheli. Usually attributed to Mauro Codussi due to "the strong typological connection" with "arrangement of the façade of Palazzo Vendarmin Calergi" (Puppi-Olivato), this building represents a moment of passage from the traditional Renaissance Venetian palaces to those influenced by central Italian traditions. The façade, inserted within an eighteen-metre square and framed vertically by angular parastas which begin at the basement and horizontally by decorated architraves with festoons, it alternates close relations between empty and full spaces which determine its unique compositional style.

"Not even in the most open gothic palaces is there such an effective contrasts between open and closed" (J. McAndrew).

The two perfectly identical upper floors are characterised by single or paired two-mullioned windows, surmounted by the "small pear-shaped instead of round window inserted in the half moon of the upper galleries" (G.Fontana) and by trefoil balconies plant. The parietal covering in smooth light-veined marble slabs combines well with the disks of red and green porphyry which give an unusual lightness which is further increased by the ashlar work, which was a new element for that period, used as a texture. As regards modifications to the interior, it seems that only simple restoration and decorative work was carried out. Nine oil paintings were commissioned from Giorgio Vasari for a richly furnished room with engraved and gilt wood; unfortunately nothing remains today and the perspective panels and the foreshortened figures, which influenced the pictorial history of Venice and in particular Veronese and Tintoretto, belong to several collections.

In 1740 the palace was apparently rented to the Spinelli family, rich silk merchants from Castefranco, while in 1810 it was purchased by Cornoldi and in 1850 it came into the hands of the ballerina, Maria Taglioni who added side balconies to the small stairway at the entrance, removing them from Ca' d'Oro, at that time being restored and also her property. Today it belongs to the Salom family.

Above: the fire-place, work of Jacopo Sansovino.

Opposite: the façade of Mauro Codussi on Canal Grande.

Pages 96-97: the lobby at the ground floor with the staircase which takes to the noble floor.

Palazzo Correr Contarini Zorzi

The Correr family arrived from Torcello at the beginning of the 9th and was indicated by Doge Pietro Gradenigo in 1927 as one of the families which should belong to the Higher Council by hereditary right. Among its members we should recall Pietro Correr, who became archbishop of Candia and the patriarch of Constantinople and a certain Angelo, who in 1406 became Pope with the name of Gregorio XII, "abdicating" shortly afterwards to become a simple cardinal. Antionio Correr also lived and died here. He is recalled as the last of the noblemen who refused to wear a wig, in that era an act which was considered to reveal a lack of seriousness and reliability. The current palace, also known as Ca' dei Cuori due to the shape of its iron coat-of-arms over the two water gates, was built in the 17th century and has an unusual façade in terms of the non-central position of the hall's three-mullioned window. The symmetry of the two water gates is not respected in terms of the upper floors, marked by marble bands which link the base, the capitals, the cornices of the squares, the balconies, the window-sills and the string-courses.

In 1771 it became the property of the Contarini family and subsequently passed to the Zorzi family.

The façade of the seventeenth-century.

Palazzo d'Anna

Commissioned in the 16th century by the Florentine family Talenti, the palace was almost immediately purchased by the rich Flemish merchant Martino d'Anna, a close friend of Tiziano Vecellio. The building, subsequently extended to the left, is of surprising simplicity: in truth the surface wall, on which the few architectural elements such as the central four-mullioned window with decorated round arch alongside the two one-light windows separated by a large coat-of-arms in relief, was designed to be decorated by Pordenone.
It is said that even Michelangelo went to Venice in order to admire its beauty and, according to Vasari "he liked it more than the whole city of Venice, and thus Pordenone was the most praised man ever to have worked in the city". An anonymous drawing held in the Victoria and Albert Museum in London allows the composition to be summarised: over the door there was a representation of *The Rape of Persephone*; between the lower side windows the *Rape of the Sabine Women* and *Marco Curzio in front of a chasm*;

on the main floor there was *Mercury in flight* and *Sybil in a flying* carriage.
From the end of eighteenth century up to the present day the palace has changed owner several times: from Viario to Foscarini and to Martinengo. At the beginning of the twentieth century it was purchased by Count Giuseppe Volpi of Misurata, a politician and important industrialist, a strong supporter of the creation of the Porto Maghera industrial area.

The façade of the sixteenth-century.

Palazzo Dandolo

This ogival palace in gothic style was built in the 14th century following a commission of the Dandolo family, along the banks of the Schiavoni, so-called because the Dalmatian sailors of "Schiavonia" moored their boats and ships here. The property was immediately divided among the female components of the family and in 1536 a part was purchased by the Gritti family to then pass to the Bernardo, Mocenigo and Nani families.

The society chronicles of the era recall it for the many parties and famous personalities who lived there; in 1530 the election of the King of Hungary and Bohemia as King of the Romans was celebrated and in 1629 the Mocenigo family, whose coat-of-arms is still recognisable in certain rooms, celebrated the marriage between Giustiniana Mocenigo and Lorenzo Giustinian there, having the *Abduction of Persephone* by Giulio Strozzi performed, one of the first musical dramas realised in Venice.

In 1822 the palace was purchased by Giuseppe dal Niel, known as Danieli, who transformed it into what is today considered one of the most prestigious hotels in the city.

Tranquillo Orsi was responsible for the architectural intervention and neo-medieval style decoration of the interior; the tall atrium has a remarkable great gilt staircase which, together with the galleries with their Moorish arches and the oriental-style pillars become a nostalgic and decadent icon of a Venice which is the destination of increasing international tourism. Among the distinguished guests of Danieli we should recall George Sand and Alfred de Musset, Marcel Proust, Honoré de Balzac, Percy Shelley and almost all the European royalty.

In 1948 a modern extension was added to the hotel: its construction led to much controversy, as in the area on which the new building stands it had not been possible to build anything more than one floor tall since 1102 when Doge Vitale Michiel was killed there.

Above: the frontage on the basin of San Marco.

Opposite: the entrance-hall rearranged according to the neoclassical-medieval taste of the middle of nineteenth-century.

Palazzo Falier Canossa

The current appearance of the palace is due to the modifications made to the original gothic style in the middle of the 15th century. The façade is organised in an unusual way; indeed the presence of two picturesque avant-corps which flank the central pointed arch five-mullioned window, the last surviving proof of the extensive covered open galleries – 'liagò' in Venetian dialect – where much of family life took place, lead to the façade being placed back from the Canal Grande. The gothic palace was commissioned by the Falier family and it remained their property until the last century when this old family died out. The Faliers, from Fano, gave the Venetian Republic several important political and military figures; there are traces of this family from 1084 when Vitale Falier ordered the construction of the church of San Vidal. It was during his dogate that body of Saint Mark was found, the event being illustrated by Tintoretto in one large canvasses for the Scuola Grande dell'Evangelista. Giovanni Falier is today recalled for started Antonio Canova on his studies. Canova was a kitchen servant in the Falie villa at Predazzi near Asolo and he was noticed for his skill in carving a lion-decoration on the butter.

In 1492 the owner of the palace, Francesco Falier, was banished to Cyprus for life – but he returned home sooner – for having proposed a bill involved a subsidy of one hundred ducats to each impoverished nobleman: as there were at least one thousand two hundred of them, such a bill would have involved the collapse of the Republic in financial terms. However perhaps the most notorious figure remains Marino Falier, who was discovered while planning a conspiracy to overthrow the institutions and gain absolute power: he was decapitated on 7 April 1355 at the top of a staircase in the Palazzo Ducale.

The façade animated by the two characteristics projecting "liagò".

Pages 106-107: mirrors and precious golden inlays envidied the dining-room of the Palazzo.

Palazzo Giustinian

According to popular tradition, in the 12th century it was the Morosini and Falier families which rescued the Giustinian family from extinction, as all the male heirs had died during the war against the Emperor of the Orient, Emanuele Comneno.

Pope Alessandro III was begged to release the last of the Giustinian family, a young man who had become a priest in San Nicolò of Lido, from his vows so that he could get married. Giustinian then married Anna, who was the daughter of Doge Vitale II Michiel. The couple, after having produced twelve children, nine sons and three daughters, retired from society; he chose a contemplative life while his wife became a nun at the convent of Sant'Adriano of Costanziaca, which she had founded.

Palazzo Giustinian is made up of two different buildings and it was built by the middle of the 15th century, probably by Giovanni and Bartolomeo Bon. Probably for logistical reasons linked to the site, the borders and to domestic requirements, leading to the need for two courtyards and two staircases, the façade of the palace lacks the architectural balance obtained in the same period in Palazzo Bembo. The extremities of the façade are closed with corner stones in Istria stone but it does not succeed in unifying the two residential units, whose façades are perceived as separate units, clearly constructed symmetrically on a central axis. On the ground floor this becomes more than a purely architectural axis, but also a structural feature: the large water gate indeed joins together the Canal Grande with the street that separates the two buildings immediately behind the façade using a portico. The windows of each building are symmetrically distributed over the smaller water-portal, with the exception of the many lancet window on the main floor.

This magnificent example of a six-mullioned window with curved arch surmounted by quatrefoil openwork is indeed shifted towards the centre. Moreover two larger one-light windows with marble under-arch septum embellished with small hanging arches come together to "create a more compact and continuous architectural style" (Franzoi) which tries to unify the two façades.

In the first decades of the nineteenth century the palace was purchased by the painter Natale Schiavoni who created exhibition rooms for an important collection of works of art. Among important figures who lived there we should mention Richard Wagner, who spent seven months in the palace, composing the opera *Tristan and Isolda* there, and the novelist William Dean Howells.

Today it is the property of the Brando-Bardolin Counts, from Friuli.

The *continuum* architectonical of the façade on Canal Grande.

Palazzo Giustinian Lolin

In his will made on 25 June 1623, Giovanni Lolin donated his palace in San Vidal, located between Calle Vitturi and Calle Giustinian, which faced onto the Canal Grande, to his grandson Giovanni Giustinian, who was son of his daughter Franceschina, on the condition that his descendants adopt the Lolin surname.

The palace, built between the end of the fourteenth century and the beginning of the fifteenth century, probably over an existing older building, was subjected to major intervention in terms of renovation-rebuilding during the first part of the 17th century. Work was already at an advanced stage at the time of the will and Giovanni followed the work personally . However Giovanni died suddenly in 1624.

The work, commissioned from the young Venetian architect Baldassare Longhena, who in the same period was also dealing with the Widmann-Rezzonico palace, also on the Canal Grande and the façade of the church of Santa Giustina in Padua, continued without interruption and probably ended after a few years. Longhena did not intervene significantly in terms of the palace's layout and the distribution of its windows and doors. The intervention was carried out only to modernise the palace, with respect for the original gothic scheme of the building, retaining the proportions of one-light and several-light windows and the absence of the mezzanine floor,. The young Longhena, stylistically very close to Scamozzi and Serlio, used flattened parastades for the windows and the ashlar-work similar to that used by Scamozzi for the façade of Palazzo Contarini dei Scrigni.

The gothic façade is retained but presented in a completely new way, transforming the palace but leaving the structure unaltered: the façade in Istria stone with central three-mullioned central-arch-window and arched windows at the sides, almost creating five-mullioned windows, the centralised moulding and the keystones of the side lateral windows, the smooth white marble linked to the smooth band under the upper coping. The only real decoration is the series of small festoons, again in Istria stone, placed on the Corinthian capitals of the second floor three-mullioned central-arch window. The floors are emphasised and separated by recurrent cornices with balconies scarcely evident; only the central balcony on the first floor projects further in order to disguise the sweep of the façade.

The intention of the architect is clear in the composition of the palace. He tries not to move away from Venetian taste, to the extent that Selvatico states: "It seems that Longhena regrets so many fanciful eccentricities (…) where for sure there is no beauty, but at least awkwardness does not triumph."

Palazzo Giustinian Lolin was purchased by the ballerina Maria Taglioni and subsequently by Duchess Maria Luisa di Borbone Artois, who died there in 1864.

The palace was then bought by the banker Ugo Levi, great lover of music and collector of scores: together with his wife Olga, they hosted the most important music salon of the period. A frequent visitor to Levi's house was the poet Gabriele D'Annunzio, who was probably more taken with the beauty of Olga Levi, who was incorruptible, who was called Venturina by D'Annunzio, a name that came from "avventurina" a typical glass from of Murano full of glints and very difficult to create.

Today the palace houses the Ugo and Olga Levi Musical Foundation; it is still in very good condition and the interior contains a furniture in seventeenth century taste.

The elegant façade of Longhena.

Palazzo Giustinian Morosini

The palace is a big building from the late gothic period which was probably built around 1474 for the noble Giustinian family. The building is characterised by two upper floors with large windows surrounded by denticulate frames. Along the coping there is a balustrade occupying the entire terrace, including and joining together the building which was subsequently added, originally separated from the main building by a narrow street, subsequently closed, probably in 1483, by a wall with superimposed arches. The first patriarch of Venice, Lorenzo Giustiniani lived in this magnificent residence for a short period in 1432; his portrait, painted by Gentile Bellini, is very famous.

In the 17th century the palace belonged to the Morosini family who restored the interior and part of the decoration is still conserved. In the nineteenth century it became the famous Hotel Europa, visited by several important figures such as Marcel Proust, René de Chateaubriand and Stendhal. At present it is used for offices.

The gothic façade on Canal Grande.

Palazzo Grassi

On the left: the majestic covered entrance-hall.

Opposite: the façade started by Longhena and finished by Massari.

in 1722. The building has an irregular layout, as is common in Venice; in this case it is trapezoidal with the longest base along the Canal Grande. The layout recalls other similar land-based buildings and Sansovino's Ca' Corner, with the rooms situated not along the 'pòrtego' but around a central courtyard, with colonnade and open gallery on the first floor. The atrium, courtyard and staircase are on the same line, which is an extension of the entrance from the Canal Grande. Massari took his inspiration for the large pincer-shaped staircase from the drawings by Longhena for Ca' Pesaro. The walls of the staircase are decorated with frescoes by Michelangelo Morlaiter representing figures in Venetian society, masked or

The Grassi Family, which came from Bologna, was admitted to the aristocracy following the payment of 60,000 ducats in 1718, together with other families, in order to meet the financial needs of the Republic caused by the Morea war and the conquest of the Peloponnese. Angelo Grassi commissioned the palace from the architect Giorgio Massari. The main façade faces onto the Canal Grande one side onto Campo San Samuele; Giorgio Massari was already employed in the completion of the monumental Ca' Rezzonico on the opposite bank. Massari started the work on Palazzo Grassi in 1748, but he died in December 1766 before work was completed.
After an interruption, construction was completed

The blind open gallery, on the staircase, decorated with Michelangelo Morlaiter frescoes.

with costumes, resting or looking out from false balconies. On the ceiling there is the *Apotheosis of the Grassi Family* painted by Fabio Canal.

The external appearance of the palace, sober, clean and almost "flat" contrasts with Ca' Rezzonico on the opposite bank, with its carvings and light and shade effects. Here the façade is characterised by architectural features, which appear to be "drawn" and almost unadorned on a luminous plane which anticipates the neo-classical spirit and to a certain extent disguises the grandeur of the building, in comparison with the strong projection of Longheni's designs.

The façade adopts the traditional Venetian three-part arrangement, with the central windows gathered around the centre. On the ground floor, over which there is a mezzanine floor, two upper floors and the loft. The band along the base is in plain ashlar-work with careful carvings which clearly outline the simply and linear windows, with a three-part water gate inserted within an arrangement with a three-mullioned central-arch window.

The two upper floors differ in terms of the shape of the windows, round arches on the first floor and rectangular with curved or triangular tympanum on the second floor, highlighted by smooth pilasters with Ionic and Corinthian capitals. A band with overlying coping terminates the façade, which is completely clad in stone. When the Grassi family died out in the first half of the 19th century, the palace was inherited by the Tornielli Counts, then it became a hotel and after that a public bathing establishment set up by Francesco degli Antoni. In 1983 is has been bought by Fiat that, after a careful restoration realised by the architects Gae Aulenti and Antonio Foscari, made office for important arts exhibitions.

Palazzo Grimani

In *Venetia nobilissima* Jacopo Sansovino mentions palazzo Grimani in San Luca as one of the four most important palaces along the Canal Grande and in the same way, some centuries later, John Ruskin, mentions it in *The Stones of Venice*, as the most noble and colossal palace. Tradition has it that the palace was built as a love token: the father of a member of the Tiepolo family refused the hand of his daughter to a member of the Grimani family, because they did not have a palace facing onto the Canal Grande. Grimani therefore ordered the building of a palace which had windows bigger than the entrance door of Palace Tiepolo, which was almost opposite. Girolamo Grimani, who was a magistrate and knight of San Marco, commissioned an architect from Verona, Michele Sanmicheli, to build a palace which would reflect the richness and the power of the owner. Work started in 1561 and was completed in 1575, following the death of Sanmicheli, who was first replaced by Guglielmo de' Grigi from Bergamo, and then by Gian Antonio Rusconi.

The façade is divided into three in the traditional way with strong horizontal bands and is marked by a series of three-mullioned central-arch windows. The ground floor is made up of an enormous triumphal arch-portal, with at the side *Two Victories*, relief carvings by Alessandro Vittoria. The large arch leads into the atrium with columns and barrel-vault, which has its origin in Roman models. The string-courses are projecting, as is the balcony which runs along the whole façade on the first floor. The ground floor is divided by fluted pilasters, while the two upper are divided by twin columns. All the columns and the pilasters have Corinthian capitals. The building represents a first and important approach of Venetian building towards the classical architecture, as if to recall that the owners were great collectors of antique objects.

The grandeur of the palace made it ideal for welcoming the many figures received by the Grimani family as guests: in 1596 a big party was held in honour of the Dukes of Mantua. On the 4 May 1597, the Bucentaur and the procession of ducal ships arrived atup Palazzo San Luca to escort Morosina Morosini, the wife of Doge Marino Grimani, up to Piazza San Marco where she was crowned as dogaressa. The feast which followed, described by Tassini with all the details and particulars, was as usual sumptuous, and became legendary throughout Italy, so much so that Pope Clemente VIII sent Morosina the *Golden Rose* donated on the death of the dogaress, in the will, to the treasury of San Marco.
After the fall of the Republic the building was purchased by the Austrian government. Today is houses the Court of Appeal.

The façade of Michele Sanmicheli.

Pages 120-121: the "pórtego" on the noble floor with the antiques portraits of the family on the walls.

Palazzo Grimani Marcello

In the area where Palazzo Grimani Marcello stands, in 1500 there was another building, probably dating back to the 12th century, which can be clearly seen in the sixteenth century plan of Venice by Jacopo de' Barbari, with the façade marked by wide with bands windows, with pointed arches over a continuous open loggia on the ground floor.

It seems that the façade and restoration works had been commissioned in the 16th century by the Grimani family "of the golden tree" from the architect Giovanni Buora, who realised the current building with its architectural and ornamental features from the late Lombard period.

The façade is completely clad with stone. On the ground floor there is a arched water gate decorated with contrasting marble medallions. The ground-floor rectangular windows are surmounted by a triangular tympanum resting on a slightly extended architrave. The first floor has a three-mullioned window with balcony with pilasters on which the elegant half-columns rest, while on the second floor, the three-

mullioned window is instead made up of free columns. All the side windows below the sill are decorated with scroll-ornaments and ribbons. The façade is divided into three, according to the style of the era, by pilasters with Corinthian capitals. Much attention was paid to the decoration of the façade, with precious marble medallions and rectangles, festoons; the corner capitals on the left are carved with an eagle with open wings on the ground floor, and a carved harpy on the first floor; it appears that all the capitals and the friezes were painted in gold, probably with reference to the name of this branch of the family. Inside a staircase led up to ballroom, which is said to have been decorated with a frieze representing Bacchanalian revelry, painted by Jacopo and Marietta Tintoretto.

During the eighteenth century the internal structure was radically modified. In the second half of the century the palace was inhabited by Piero Grimani (Doge from 1741 to 1752) who encouraged the presence of prominent figures from the Enlightenment. The last

modifications were probably made during this period by Pietro Bianchi, who was an architect and the son of the private gondolier of the "free trader" Grimani.

In the 20th century the palace passed from the Grimani Giustinian family to the current owner, Sorlini.

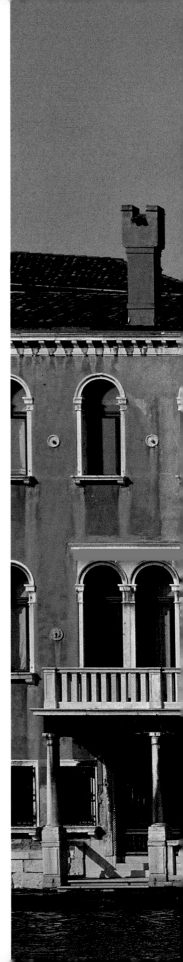

The façade tipical example of architecture of the late Lombardy-period.

Palazzo Gussoni Cavalli Franchetti

At the beginning of the sixteenth century the rich Cavalli family, from Bavaria, bought the palace of the old and noble Gussoni family. The residence is situated in an enviable position overlooking the Canal Grande and opposite the Accademia and remained the property of the Cavalli family until almost 1830. After that it was bought by Archduke Frederic of Austria, son of Archduke Karl. Frederic died when he was very young in 1847, after having been nominated as supreme commander of the Austrian navy. The palace was then bought by Enrico di Borbone Artois, Count of Chambord. Marie Terese of France, who was the surviving daughter of Luigi XVI and Marie Antoinette, was a guest of Count Chambord for many months. Baron Raimondo Franchetti bought the palace from Chambord in 1866. The grandiose building has a gothic façade with pointed arches of great beauty: the two upper floors are very similar, both in terms of height and due to the presence of two particularly attractive five-lancet windows. The lower one is decorated with an interlaced arch motif, while the upper one by half quatrefoil elements, created by the interlacing of the arches, already present in Ca' Foscari. However in comparison with Foscari palace, here the decoration is more sedate and decisive, marked by the alternation of full and empty space and the projecting coping which terminates the façade and the siting of small brackets. The balconies of the first floor project over the windows, while on the second floor they are only present in the five-lancet window and in line with the brickwork. On the first floor there are also side windows culminating with openwork quatrefoils, while on the second floor the windows are surrounded by a dentate cornice and a low-relief that closes the keystone of the gothic arch. Small twisted columns mark the corners on each floor. The façade is the result of the restoration work commissioned by Baron Franchetti from Camillo Boito who was assisted by Carlo Matscheg and Girolamo Manetti. Boito built also the majestic great staircase at the rear of the palace, taking his inspiration from a "reinterpretation of the medieval age": it is situated within in an architectural structure seems almost separate from the palace itself, lightened on the three open sides by three several lancet windows which recall the decorative motif of the façade. The fixtures are made of iron and in view, almost as if to underline the modernity of the restoration.

The interior decoration is makes use of a mixture of paintings, sculpture and applied arts. The area on the side of the palace was occupied by a boathouse which the Republic did not succeed in closing. It was finally freed by the Count of Chambod, who transformed it into the garden which can still be admired. The palace today houses the offices of a bank.

On the left: decorative detail on the façade.

Opposite: the late-gothic-period-façade on Canal Grande.

Sculptures, paintings and furniture create a rich and unitary decoration in the wide hall of passage.

Palazzo Gussoni Grimani Della Vida

The Gussoni were an old family which had already arrived in Venice by the beginning of the 9th century, when they participated in the realisation of the church of Santa Sofia. Around the middle of the sixteenth century they commissioned the restoration of the original gothic Byzantine building which resulted in the current palace from Marco Sanmicheli. The façade is tripartite, according to the traditional Venetian design: the upper floor is given emphasis by the central four-lancet window with round arches, the continuous projected balcony and the upper closing coping; the side windows are linked by a continuous upper cornice which also marks the base of the round tympanum used to decorate the windows. Two aristocratic coat-of-arms are also to be found at the level of the upper floor. The façade was decorated with fresco paintings, apparently by Jacopo Tintoretto, with various figures including *Adam and Eve, Cain and Abel* and *Twilight and Dawn*, these last inspired by the sculptures of Michelangelo in the Medici chapels in Florence. Currently no traces have remained, but there is a representation in the engravings of Antonio Maria Zanetti, published in 1760 in *Several Fresco Pictures.*

From 1647 up to 1690 the Gussoni palace was the seat of the Delfica Academy, also called the Gussonian Academy, famous for the study of the eloquence; around the middle of the eighteenth century the palace was purchased by the Grimani family and subsequently by Cesare della Vida, a rich Israeli businessman.

Nowadays the Gussoni palace is the property of the State, housing the Tax Inspectors Department.

In 1735 when Senator Giulio died, the palace was inherited by his wife Faustina and his daughter Giustiniana. She was famous the Venetian society as a result of her elopement and clandestine marriage with Count Francesco Tassis from Bergamo; however the marriage was not recognised by the Council of Ten and Giustiniana, who was soon to become a widow, returned to Venice and married Piero Maria Curti.

The façade of Sanmicheli originally frescoed as it seems by Tintoretto.

Palazzo Labia

On the left: detail of a ceiling picture with feminine figures (unknown author).

On the right: the façade of Comilelli on Cannaregio canal.

Pages 132-133: in the dancing hall the squaring of Girolamo Mengozzi Colonna frame the frescoes of Giambattista Tiepolo which represent the Histories of Antonio and Cleopatra.

The Labia were Catalan merchants who moved first to Avignon, then to Florence and finally to Venice. Here they joined the city aristocracy in 1646, following the payment of three hundred thousand ducats to support the war with Candia. Giovan Francesco Labia immediately decided to commission the construction of a palace worthy of his rank in the city and he moved to San Moisè in San Geremia, close to the Spanish Embassy.

In 1663 the building was concluded and on his death in 1665, Giovan Francesco Labia left a majestic building, later to be extended by his heirs, completing the original plan. The attribution of the design for the palace is still uncertain. The names of two architects have always been suggested: Alessandro Tremignon and Andrea Cominelli; in truth the palace was probably started by Paolo Tremignon, the son of Alessandro and also an architect, but less famous within the city; later it would appear that Cominelli concluded the work.

The sumptuous building factory has three façades: one faces onto the Canal Grande, with a central door and three windows on the various levels; one faced onto the Regio Canal (Canareggio) with a door and ten windows; the third onto Campo San Geremia. The façades adopt

On the ceiling *The Genius on Pegasus who chases away the Time* of Tiepolo.

the classical two order style of Sansovino for the two upper floors. In the attics there are round windows alternating with carved heraldic eagles. In the second half of the 18th century Paolo Antonio Labia ordered the extension of the building towards Campo San Geremia.

In the same period the most important rooms in the palace were decorated by Giambattista Tiepolo. In particular, on the walls and on ceilings of the ballroom and the two adjacent rooms, fresco paintings were realised with the figures of *Zephyrus and Flora, Bacchus and Arianna* and the story of *Antonio and Cleopatra,* one of the most important pictorial cycles by this great Venetian artist. The scenes are linked to one another by false architecture and the *trompe l'oeil* decoration of Girolamo Mengozzi Colonna, from Ferrara, who was a genuine master of this genre. In such compositions Tiepolo seems to refer to the great period of sixteenth century Venetian painting (there are clear references to Veronese in the clothes, armour and architecture). Sumptuous parties were held in the palace. It is said that at the end of the banquets the owner threw left all the gold and silver dishes used into the Cannareggio canal, accompanying this gesture saying "L'abia o non l'abia, sarò sempre Labia"(whether I have them or not I will always be a Labia). However there was a fishing net under the surface of the water which allowed the servants to recover the treasure as soon as the guests left.

After several transfers of ownership and different uses as a school and house for example, the palace, which risked losing all its fresco paintings due to the lack of care of the various owners, after the Second World War the property was acquired by Carlos de Beistegui, a fabulously rich French-Mexican collector. De Beistegui lived there for long time, furnishing the palace with antique furniture and housing his rich collection of 18th century objects d'art there. After his death the furniture and collection were dispersed, with the exception of some pieces which Nino Barbantini luckily managed to repurchase.

Since 1970 the palace, completely restored, has been home to the offices of the RAI-Italian Radio television.

Palazzo Loredan dell'Ambasciatore

The elegant palace which faces on the Canal Grande, not far from the Accademia Galleries was probably built around the middle of the 15th century in the florid late gothic period. It was built for the noble family Loredan, and its name came from the concession Doge Francesco Loredan made to the Imperial court of Austria: for twenty-nine years it housed the Imperial Embassy. Thus the Doge ceded his own private residence, but in exchange he demanded advance and complete payment of the rent and requested that restoration costs be covered by the Ambassador. The response of the court is unclear , however Ambassador Filippo di Rosemburg Orsini was alrady resident in the palace by 1754.

Previously the Loredan family had received Count Matthias von der Schulemburg as their guest for a long time. Together with Antonio Loredan, he fought and defeated the Turks in 1716, blocking their advance towards Venice. Count von Schulemburg was a great collector, friend and patron of several artists such as Giambattista Piazzetta and Antonio Guardi. When he died, his collection of pictures included almost nine hundred works of art, with pictures by Lorenzo Lotto, Caravaggio and Mantegna. The palace is clearly in late gothic style; the upper floor is adorned with a four-mullioned window, with large quatrefoil elements, a projecting balcony decorated with an elegant baluster held up by consoles, and there are pendentives on the spires of the gothic arches of the side windows; on the higher floor there is another open four-lancet window, with a small gallery set back from the façade. All the gothic windows are surrounded by dentate frames and pendentives on the spires; the small columns are surmounted by engraved capitals with leaf motifs. On the façade, between the side windows on the upper floor, there are two statues of shield-holding page-boys, placed inside marble niches in Renaissance style.

Above: an inside room.

Opposite: the late-gothic façade on Canal Grande.

Palazzo Loredan Vendramin Calergi

The palace was built in the first years of the 16th century and is considered to be one of the "main palaces along the Canal Grande" (F. Sansovino) and the first architectural example of the Renaissance renewal of the city.

In 1481 Andrea Loredan of Nicolò bought some buildings in San Marcuola and entrusted an architect from Bergamo, Mauro Codussi, who was already working for the Loredan family on the church of San Michele in Isola, with the construction of a building which was to manifest the undying grandeur of the family and of the state. It appears that not even the foundations had been completed when construction was halted as a result of legal disputes with neighbours, which were only resolved on 30 March 1502. It is curious to notice that in the xylograph of Jacopo de' Barbari in 1500 we can still see the old construction, which undoubtedly no longer existed. In 1504, when Codussi died, the façade must already have been started. "The perfect coherence of the composition of the façade" (Olivato, Puppi) suggests that

his son Domenico replaced him in directing work, although the nature of the sculptural decorations on the façade suggests the intervention of a craftsman from the Lombardo family. Still divided vertically into three according to tradition, the façade is striking for the force of the horizontal bands on the three floors and for the new magnificence obtained thanks to the abandoning of terracotta and open brickwork in favour of complete

cladding in calcareous stone. The structure of the ground floor, more compact than the upper floors, is marked by the pilasters which frame the two large windows and the great water portal; under the windows of the mezzanine floor the following inscription is engraved: NON NOBIS, DOMINE, NON NOBIS, taken from Psalm 113 (9) (which continues with SED NOMINI TUO DA GLORIAM), apparently demanded by Loredan himself as an act of humility to God

Above: an inside room of the palace that nowadays is office of the Municipal Casino.

Opposite: the façade of Codussi on Canal Grande.

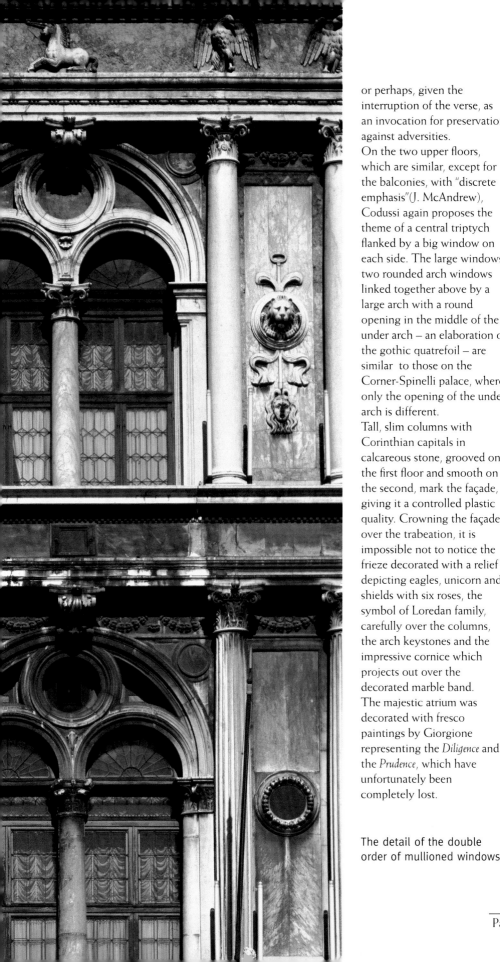

or perhaps, given the interruption of the verse, as an invocation for preservation against adversities.

On the two upper floors, which are similar, except for the balconies, with "discrete emphasis"(J. McAndrew), Codussi again proposes the theme of a central triptych flanked by a big window on each side. The large windows, two rounded arch windows linked together above by a large arch with a round opening in the middle of the under arch – an elaboration of the gothic quatrefoil – are similar to those on the Corner-Spinelli palace, where only the opening of the under arch is different.

Tall, slim columns with Corinthian capitals in calcareous stone, grooved on the first floor and smooth on the second, mark the façade, giving it a controlled plastic quality. Crowning the façade, over the trabeation, it is impossible not to notice the frieze decorated with a relief depicting eagles, unicorn and shields with six roses, the symbol of Loredan family, carefully over the columns, the arch keystones and the impressive cornice which projects out over the decorated marble band.

The majestic atrium was decorated with fresco paintings by Giorgione representing the *Diligence* and the *Prudence*, which have unfortunately been completely lost.

The detail of the double order of mullioned windows.

When Andrea died (1513) the palace was inherited by his nephews, who in 1851 sold it to the Duke of Brunswick; in 1589 was purchased by Vettor Calergi, who left in his will to his daughter Marina who married Vincenzo Grimani. In 1614 they commissioned the extension of the palace from Vincenzo Scamozzi, who constructed the so-called "white-wing" over the garden: this wing was demolished in 1658 following an order of the Council of Ten to punish the three Grimani brothers, who had killed Francesco Querini Stampalia there. In place of the building an infamous column was erected: however only two years later, the Grimani brothers succeeding in obtaining a pardon and quickly rebuilt the part of the palace which had been knocked down.

The palace was passed down and in 1738 came into the hands of Nicolò Vendramin who, thanks to a commitment of the Grimani family, added Calergi to his surname, in this way establishing the definitive name of the palace. In 1844 the building was purchased by Duchess Maria Carolina du Berry; his heirs rented a part of the palace to Richard Wagner, who died here in 1883, as poetically recalled by Gabriele D'Annunzio on a memorial tablet on the wall of the garden.

After being purchased by Count Giuseppe Volpi of Misurata, in 1946 it became the property of the Municipality, which determined its use as the municipal casino.

Palazzo Mastelli del Cammello

The palace, a little away from the usual tourist routes, at the centre of the crowded Cannaregio district, owes its name to a relief carving set into the wall of the façade, just to the right of the balcony on the first floor representing a man in oriental dress riding a camel. Traditionally it is considered the symbol of the owners, the Mastelli family, who came from the Orient, arriving in Venice in 1112, and a century later, in 1202, participated in the crusade led by Doge Enrico Dandolo. The Mastelli family were part of the rich merchant class, having had been admitted to the Higher Council, but for an unknown reason they were suddenly excluded from the Council.

The overall complex of buildings ("very honourable" as described by the chronicles of the time) which flanked Campo dei Mori, lying between the canals of the Madonna dell'Orto and Sensa canal, delimiting Palazzo Mastelli to the east, was built and was the property of the family. On the corner at the foot of the Mori bridge there are four thirteenth century statues of merchants: the first three are the brothers Mastelli, while the one on the corner is said to be Rioba, as indicated on his bundle, whereas the other two on the land are Sandi and Anfani; the one at the bottom, with a turban, does not have name. As regards the first three, in a manuscript held in the National Library Marciana in Venice it is possible to read: "(…) three large marble figures dressed in Greek style, (…) they carry bundles on their backs, in the shape of a suitcase, perhaps to demonstrate the wealth they brought to Venice" (VII class, manuscript 27, National Library of Marciana, Venice). They were called Mori (Moor) as a result of their origin, and this name was also given to area opposite. The most important features of on the façade are the ogival central gallery on the second floor, enriched with quatrefoils and a dentate frame, the corner two-lancet windows, again on the second floor, which recall the windows of Palazzo Priuli and a squat column, standing in the corner window on the first floor.

Above: high-relief which represents the camel that gives the name to the palace.

Opposite: the façade on Rio della Madonna dell'Orto.

Palazzo Michiel delle Colonne

The name of the palace comes from the architectural structure on the ground floor, with an extended arcade running along the whole façade, made uup of tall columns and linked to each other by round arches with central arch window in the middle.

The Zen family bought the palace, which is in Venetian Byzantine style (as confirmed by several drawings), around the end of the 17th century from the Grimani family and commissioned its renovation from Antonio Gaspari, who on the façade essentially limited himself superimposing the old structure with new ornamentation and curved tympanums, interrupted in the centre by busts on consoles, to decorate the windows. Gaspari then gave the same architectural importance to the two upper floors by using the same three-mullioned central-arch-window. The only traces of the previous building are to be found in the internal courtyard.

Shortly after the renovation by Gaspari, the palace was purchased by Ferdinanado Carlo Gonzaga, Duke of Mantua. In 1707 the Austrians conquered the Lombard city and the Duke hid in Venice in this very palace, where he had previously transferred a part of his several artistic collections: antique furniture, majolica ware and porcelain, which are now to be found at the Correr Museum, paintings such as the *Pietà* and the *Madonna with Child between John the Baptist and a Saint* by Giovanni Bellini (at present in the Accademia Galleries) and a very important painting attributed to Giorgione (nowadays in a private collection).

The palace was then purchased by the Michiel family. In 1716 it received as a guest Frederic II, Elector of Saxony and subsequently King of Poland. In the house on the Canal Grande the Republic organised a series of spectacles and feasts in honour of another famous guest, the Elector of Bavaria, Karl Albert. In the nineteenth century the palace belonged to the Martinengo family and subsequently the Donà delle Rose family.

Today the palace houses the registry offices.

The façade on the Canal Grande characterised by the disproportionate columns of the round floor.

Palazzo Mocenigo Casa Nuova

In the palace on the far left of the large complex of buildings belonging to the Mocenigo family, a second branch of the family resided, originally from Milan. Probably by 1579, the building was restored to adequately welcome Alvise I Mocenigo, Doge in the period of the victory of the Venetian Republic in Lepanto. In the same year the Mocenigo family restored their residences at San Stae and the Giudecca. The reconstruction plan has been variously attributed by historians to Guglielmo dei Grigi, Da Ponte, Rusconi and Andrea Palladio, but it was probably Alessandro Vittoria from Trento who followed the design: there are strong similarities with Palazzo Balbi, situated on the other bank of the Canal Grande, right opposite Palazzo Mocenigo and certainly designed by him, in terms of the architectural distribution of the design project. Vittoria did not neglect the lessons learnt from Palladio in terms of constructional and decorative devices, as we can indeed see in the central-arch superimposed windows, in the curved tympanum windows alternating with triangular tympanum windows and in the way that the materials are used. The two upper floors are marked by the continuous galleries of the central arched windows. All the architectural elements on the façade are framed by cornices and profiles which delineate the walls. The last floor was terraced much later, to create a private attic. In general the layout is relatively traditional, except for the use of several staircases in the interior. The huge hall and the majestic proportions of the main staircase would suggest that the palace was reconstructed with the idea of giving large parties and important receptions.

Here indeed Pisana Cornaro Mocenigo welcomed the Polish King Frederic

On the left: foreshortening of the large hall.

Opposite: the façade of the late sixteenth-century attributed to Alessandro Vittoria.

The large hall on the noble floor.

Augustus III in 1716 with a major ceremony. Throughout Italy and Europe people spoke for a long time of the sumptuousness and the splendour of the party given in his honour.
The Mocenigo family had important art collections and loved to be surrounded by artists; one of the ceilings in the palace was painted by Giambattista Tiepolo between 1755 and 1757 with "The dawn dissipating the clouds of the night" – now at the Museum of Fine Arts in Boston.

Palazzo Mocenigo Casa Vecchia

Constructed in the nineteenth century, historically it was the first property of the Mocenigo in San Manuele.

It was rebuilt by Francesco Contin between 1623 and 1625 (this information is given by E.A. Cicogna in *Delle iscrizioni Veneziane*, published in Venice in 1824 – 1853; Vittoria was able to consult a summary of commissioning costs). The building is simple and linear: a ground floor without mezzanine floor, two upper floors perfectly similar in terms of height and proportion (the only difference is the balcony of the three-lancet projecting windows in the centre). The arches are marked by heads on keystone.

Numerous famous guests were lodged in the two Mocenigo palaces on Canal Grande, among whom Giordano Bruno, who was denied hospitality and denounced to the Inquisition in fear of clerical and secular power. The friar was then conducted to Rome, condemned as a heretic and burned alive in Campo de' Fiori.

The two Mocenigo palaces, Casa Vecchia and Casa Nuova, were joined together by two smaller palaces, whose main façade and courtyard were decorated with frescoes by Benedetto Caliari and Giussepe Alabardi on a Roman theme: unfortunately the only evidence of these is the print published by Luca Carlevarijs in 1703.

The poet Thomas Moore stayed in Palazzo Mocenigo, and for more than a year Lord Byron rented numerous rooms in the two smaller buildings: here the English poet wrote the first two canticles of *Don Juan*. The façades of the two small palaces faced over the Canal Grande and were completely decorated with frescoes, as can be seen in a print by Luca Carlevarijs.

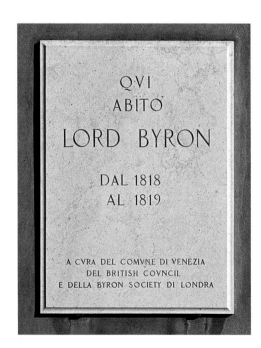

On the left: the tablet that remembers the Venetian stay of Lord Byron on the frontage of the contiguous palace which belongs always to Mocenigo's family.

On the right: the façade renewed by Contin in the first decennium of the seventeenth-century.

Palazzo Moro-Lin

The palace called "with thirteen windows" is the result of the restoration of two neighbouring palaces. The space which divided the two original palaces probably corresponds with the large central window. Palazzo Moro Lin was erected in 1670, according to a design by the Tuscan painter Sebastiano Mazzoni, best known as a painter rather than for his sporadic activities as an architect. The palace was created according to a certain antique taste: long and low, it was perhaps inspired by the Florentine Palazzo Pitti. The façade is entirely decorated with ashlar - work with continuous windows interspersed with pilasters with capitals.

The last floor is the result of subsequent restoration work, which took place after the wedding between Gaspare Moro and Isabella Lin.

The first owner and purchaser of the palace was Pietro Liberi, a painter with a somewhat adventurous life. Originating from Padua, after a period of training in a workshop in Padua, he left for Constantinople, were he was captured by the Turks and made a slave. After many months of captivity, he escaped from the Turks and landed in Malta, then in Sicily, wandering around Europe to eventually arrive in Venice; here he established the successful College of Painters, an association of artists which later became part of the Accademia.

In 1691 the palace became the property of the Lin family, who were merchants from Bergamo and who joined the Venetian nobility in 1686 following the payment of a sum of money. In the eighteenth century the interior of the palace was richly decorated by Liberihimself, but also by Antonio Molinari, Antonio Bellucci and Luca Carlevarijs. In the nineteenth century it was redecorated by Carlo Bevilacqua and Pietro Moro. At the beginning of the nineteenth century the Venetian painter Francesco Hayez studied here, and subsequently another painter, Ludovico Lipparini.

Lipparini acquired a large part of the establishment and held pictorial academies here frequented by artists from all over Europe.

The long façade measured by the famous thirteen windows.

Palazzo Morosini Brandolin

The palace, overlooking the Canal Grande opposite Ca' d'Oro, was build by the Morisini family at the beginning of the 15th century. The Morosini were a branch of the San Cassiano family. The façade has two upper floors, (a third upper floor was demolished around the middle of the 19th century, while in the same period the second floor was divided in two in terms of height, creating new residential units, more in line with the times) characterised by two beautiful six-lancet windows with magnificent cornices. The several light window on the first floor has rosettes at the tops of the arches and a projecting balcony resting on corbels, while the second floor window is decorated with openwork quatrefoils between the arches.
To the side of the several light windows there are two series of windows with pointed arches with rosettes at the tops: these too are surrounded by dentate cornices.
Ashlar-work in Istria stone of alternating size and twisted columns are sited at the corners closing the façade.
The ground floor was modified in the 19th century and is clad in white marble. "In terms of its grandeur and perhaps the distribution of the windows, the palace would appear to emulate Palazzo Ca' Foscari" (Edoardo Arslam).
Palazzo Brandolin is now divided into private apartments and cannot be visited.

The gothic façade on Canal Grande.

Palazzo Morosini Sagredo

On the left: detail of the small lion on the balcony of the palace.

Opposite: the façade of the fourteenth-century period building.

Gherardo Sagredo, the great–grandson of Doge Nicolò who died in 1676, purchased the palace in Santa Sofia from the Morosini family at the beginning of the eighteenth century, beginning modernisation work immediately. Sagredo was married to Cecilia Grimani Calergi and had two daughters. One daughter married a Pisani and the other a member of the Barbarigo family. In his will, Gherardo established that the palace of Santa Sofia would go to the Sagredo branch of the family, who were richer, thus hoping that the restoration and improvement work would be completed. The palace was constructed between the 12th and the 14th centuries, as can bee seen in the windows of the mezzanine floor, when the sic-light window was probably centrally placed on the façade. The right wing and the trefoil windows were added subsequently added, fashionable in the period and probably deriving from the design of Palazzo Ducale, which was being constructed in the same period. The four-lancet window on the upper floor is remarkable, framed by an elaborate frieze and adorned with polychrome patera made in precious marbles.

The façade was decorated with frescoes (as can be seen in the lithography of the palace by M.Moro in 1865) and this contributed to giving a sense of unity to the whole magnificent complex. Modernisation work began on the interior, the attic floor being enhanced by the decoration of the craftsmen Carpoforo Mazzetti Tencalla and Abbondio Stazio, who almost totally covered it with

elegant stucco-work.
At the bottom of the atrium Sagredo constructed the sumptuous staircase, which in 1734 was completely covered with fresco decoration by Pietro Longhi on the theme of the *Fall of the Giants* probably inspired by the frescoes of Giulio Romano in Palazzo Te in Mantua.
For Longhi this fresco was an isolated example in his pictorial career, a fact which demonstrates the importance and consideration attributed

to the purchaser and the palace in the city. Restoration of the palace took place under the guidance of Andrea Tirali and he is probably responsible for joining the sidewall overlooking Campo Santa Sofia, which in the famous plan of Venice by Jacopo De'Barbari (1500), shows the side interrupted by a courtyard, probably with an uncovered staircase. The work decided by Gherardo also provided for the renovation of the façade,

assigned to Temanza, as demonstrated by drawings published in *Admiranda Urbis Venetae*, but this work was not implemented, despite the provisions of Sagredo's will. On the death of Gherardo, the palace was soon deprived of its rich art collections, sold to private individuals and museums; in 1906 the Metropolitan Museum of New York bought a particularly beautiful bed decorated with Cupids in full relief.

Above: the gothic arcs and trilobated of the four-mullioned window anticipate the characteristics of the late gothic mullioned-windows.

Opposite: the majestic eighteenth century staircase, work of Tirali, is "completed" by the Falls of the Giants of Pietro Longhi.

Pages 160-161: the noble floor is characterised by paintings realized by Andrea Urbani in 1773.

Palazzo Pesaro degli Orfei Fortuny

This large palace, isolated from other buildings in the area, was built around the end of the 15th century by the powerful ancient Pesaro family: according to legend, they descended directly from Jove.

The palace has three façades: one faces onto Campo San Beneto, the other onto Calle Pesaro and the last onto the Ca' Michiel canal.

The façade facing onto Campo San Beneto is one of the most complex in the gothic venetian period, with two large six-lancet windows in the centre, a wing on the left-hand side with the windows situated away from the central ones and a wing on the right-hand side with the windows instead close to the many-light window. On the ground floor the main door is situated alongside small pointed windows.

The corners are marked by ashlar – work in Istria stone, in different sizes, alternating with twisted columns.

The other two façades were also impressive: the one overlooking the canal is severe and sober, marked by the several-light window on the first and second floors, while the third floor has a shortened four-lancet

window. On the ground floor there is a water gate surrounded by four windows. Other several-light windows were necessarily constructed over the main courtyard, as the enormous depth of the first and second floors prevented the light coming from the seven-lancet from reaching the courtyard. The palace is perhaps the symbol of the venetian – gothic

Above: foreshortening of the inside courtyard.

Opposite: the access in the "pórtego" on the first noble floor.

Pages 164-165-166-167: the rooms are completely furnished with precious curtains, materials and drapes made by Mariano Fortuny y Madrazo himself (pages 166-167).

sumptuousness, dictated by the importance of the families commissioning properties, both in terms of the size of the palace and the decorative solutions adopted: the balconies of the several-light windows are held up by lions in Lombard style and the other balconies by architrave balusters with a frieze of fifteenth century cherubs.

In the sixteenth century the Pesaro family organised numerous theatrical and musical spectacles and dances and parties inside the palace and the courtyards.

In the 18th century, with the construction of another palace, Palazzo Pesaro on the Canal Grande, the family moved away, leaving the residence in Campo San Benedetto to the Accademia Filarmonica degli Orfei, which continued to organise concerts and balls, until it moved into the Gran Teatro La Fenice.

At the beginning of the twentieth century the palace was acquired by Mariano Fortuny y Madrazo, an aristocratic and eclectic Spanish artist (Granada 1871 - Venice 1949), who created his art studio in the palace. Despite the neo-gothic trends in the era, Fortuny did not make any structural alterations to the palace, so it remained very similar to the way it was when it was constructed: only precious curtains, materials and drapes made by Fortuny himself used to change the arrangement of the rooms. Fortuny was a very versatile artist, a scene designer, painter, inventor and craftsman. He rediscovered the weaving of cloth in the ancient Venetian manner with golden and silver yarn: his clothes, light as feathers, were worn by Eleonora Duse, Isadora Duncan and Sarah Bernhard. In his palace – workshop he invented the Dome, a sort of starry theatrical backdrop, which is still used in many theatres in order to give the idea of the depth of the sky.

In 1956 the palace became the property of the Municipal government of Venice.

Palazzo Pisani

The Pisani family were important bankers indeed known as the "Dal Banco" family, who in the 15th century established an exchange bank in the Rialto. In the following century a part of the family decided to settle down in Santo Stefano. Alvise Pisani had this magnificent residence built (perhaps according to one of his own ideas and with the assistance of Bartolomeo Manopola, then supervisor at the Palazzo Ducale).

It was constructed between Campiello, next to Campo Santo Stefano and the Santissimo canal. For the construction of this palace, the Pisani family spent 200,000 ducats, an enormous sum for the time.

However the history of the palace is full of gaps. The chronicles narrate that the palace was built between 1614 and 1615. A few years later, in 1634, it suffered serious damage as the result of an earthquake.

In the following years the palace had only one upper floor, while the wing facing the Canal Grande was lacking, as can be seen in reproductions of period prints by Carlevanjs in Coronelli.

From 1668 to 1716, the Pisani family purchased some neighbouring buildings and in 1728, the architect Girolano Frigimelica was entrusted with the assignment to extend the Santo Stefano palace.

He was also commissioned to design the huge residence for the Pisani family at Stra in Venice, on the Brenta River. Respecting the symmetry of the palace's structure, the architect added a second upper floor and a crowning floor, using an arched window from a demolished attic as the central window. He also created a new wing with a new library and ballroom; a façade over the narrow canal was also erected, destined to remain of secondary importance also as a result of restrictions in terms of funds, due to expenses for the construction of the villa in Stra.

The façade of the palace facing over Campo Santo Stefano, as we see it today, follows the traditional tripartite pattern: at the centre of the ground floor there is a large entrance, while the two upper floors are marked by two large central–arched windows. At the sides the arched windows have a head carved onto the keystone of the arch, with a slender column at their centre, while to the sides they are closed with pilasters. The first floor balcony is projects slightly and is supported by two big modillions which extend up to the main entrance; the balcony is decorated with a finely cut baluster with a square motif.

The whole façade is clad with ashlar-work in light coloured stone which on the ground floor also delineates the windows, underlining the modernity of the building's design,

The layout is also unusual for Venice: the most evident feature is the two internal courtyards, separate and linked together at the same time by a structure four floors high with open galleries, creating an elegant and wall-screen.

The palace stretches towards the Canal Grande, with a narrow wing which, when it was finished in 1751 had a small and sober side façade. The interior of the palace was richly decorated by some of the most well-known Venetian painters: Giacomo Guarana, Jacopo Amigoni, Sebastiano Ricci, Pittoni and Gian Domenico Tiepolo. Palazzo Pisani was also the scene of memorable celebrations, particularly in honour of Gustav III of Sweden, who on his departure admitted that he would never be able to match the hospitality he had received.

Since 1940 the municipality government of Venice has owned the property, which after major restoration work, now houses the Benedetto Marcello conservatoire.

The façade on "campiello" Pisani in Santo Stefano.

Palazzo Pisani Gritti

The palace, the property of the Pisani "Dal Banco" family, was probably constructed around the middle of the 15th century, although Edoardo Arslam (*Venezia Gotica* 1970) attributes to a century earlier. The façade on the Canal Grande is marked by two five-lancet windows surrounded by dentate frames. The first floor has projecting balconies both for the main five-lancet and the lateral windows.

The corners of the façade, as was typical in gothic Venetian buildings, are marked by Istria stone quoins in different sizes, and by twisted columns.

Unfortunately the fresco decoration by Giorgione on the façade has completely disappeared.

At the beginning of the 19th century the palace was subjected to radical modernisation work: indeed the last floor was substantially raised, giving greater living space.

Palazzo Pisani was purchased in 1814 by Camillo Gritti, a descendant of noble and ancient Venetian family. Indeed in 1104 a certain Giovanni Gritti who was a captain at the battle of Acri,

The façade of the middle fifteenth century seems to be painted by Giorgine.

while Andrea Gritti was
perhaps one of the greatest
Venetian Doges in the
sixteenth century, after
having been first a merchant
and then a leader during the
Cambrian league and
subsequently Ambassador of
the Republic.
In the nineteenth century the
Gritti family sold the palace
to Baroness Susanna Wetzlar,
John Ruskin staying with her
in 1851 while he was
dedicating himself to *The stone
of Venice.* The palace was
subsequently transformed
into a luxury Hotel: among
the most assiduous and
famous visitors there was the
writer Ernest Hemingway
and in more recent times the
producer Woody Allen.

Palazzo Pisani Moretta

This important building on Canal Grande was built around the middle of the 15th century by the Bembo family, who decided to modify the exterior, realising the building as it is today, according to the typical configuration of later Venetian gthic style.

With the traditional tripartite structure delimited by pilasters in Renaissance style, the façade is made up of the ground floor, with a double water gate which emphasis the use of the palace by two families, and of two upper floors; the balustrade and the addition of the last floor are modifications made in the nineteenth century.

The palace's rigorous composition is characterised by the rich quatrefoil decorations of the two central six-lancet windows. These recall the airy mullioned windows of Palazzo Ducale's upper floors, offering a structural variant with pointed arches, while on the second floor they are placed at the intersection of the round arches. Little is known about the history of the palace before 1629, the year in which it was ceded by Agnesia Renier to Francesco Pisani Moretta. The Moretta branch of the Pisani family were among the most ancient and richest families in the Venetian aristocracy. They only came to reside in the palace in 1670. They descended from Nicolò Pisani, who from 1307 to 1328 was a member of the Major Council.

The "Pisani dal Banco" family, whose name derived from their main activity, banking and trade, descended from Bertucci (Alberto, whereas the "Santo Stefano", "Santa Maria Zobenigo" and "Moretta" Pisanis (this last branch taking their name from the repetitive use of the name Almorò – Almoretto) descended from the other son, Amoro (Ermolao). The last descendent of this family, the attorney Francesco Pisani Moretta, known as Pietro, died in 1737 leaving the palace to his daughter Chiara in his will. She married one of the "Pisani Dal Banco" branch, guaranteeing the continuity of the name. Chiara inherited a palace which was in serious state of decay, but she also inherited a lot of money, the fruit of the many economies made by her father, worried about his financial position, money which allowed her undertake a radical restoration of the building.

In the courtyard giving access from the land the external gothic staircase was demolished in order to construct the sober internal staircases with facing flights which lead up to the 'pòrtego', transformed into a ballroom, according to a design by Andrea Tirali. The sober monumental character of the first staircase contrasts with the magnificent decoration of the other staircase. The rich polychrome stucco decoration, carried out subsequently by Ferrari and Castelli in *Rocaille* style, and Guarana's frescoes representing *Light defeating darkness and Apollo in the early hours* are still only illuminated by the light of the candles in the imposing Murano glass chandeliers which are reflected in the large mirrors enclosed in gilt stucco frames. However before Guarana, other important artists were called on to work in other rooms within the palace.

In 1743 Giambattista Tiepolo painted the ceiling of one of the rooms on the upper floor with *The meeting between Venus and Mars*. Between 1745 and 1746 *The death of Dario* now at Ca' Rezzonico was commissioned from to

The late-gothic façade on Canal Grande.

On the left: particular of Giambattista Tiepolo fresco, which represents *The apotheosis of the admiral Vettor Pisani.*

On the right: the majestic staircase introduces in the "pórtego" of the noble floor.

Pages 178-179: the "pórtego", sumptuous receiving-room with a Jacopo Guarana fresco on the ceiling.

Gianbattista Piazzetta, to match the famous picture by Paolo Veronese *the Dario family at Alessandro's feet* today at the National Gallery in London. In 1753 Vettor, one of Chiara's sons, had an affair with Teresa Dalla Vedova, a young lady belonging to the city's middle class and they were married in secret. When the secret was discovered, Teresa was sent to a convent, where after a short time she gave birth to her son Pietro, who was not recognised by his father. After Vettor's death, his son Pietro filed a suit against the family, winning the case and becoming a member of the Pisani family and receiving a part of the assets, together with the title of Count of Bagnolothus becoming a member of the Venetian nobility. In 1847, on the death of Pietro Pisani the palace was inherited by his son Vettor Daniele, the last male descendant, whom then left the palace to one of his three daughters, who had married a member of the Giusti family. The palace, perfectly restored and conserved, still belongs to their heirs.

Palazzo Priuli all'Osmarin

The Priuli family were a noble Hungarian family, who arrived in Venice as diplomats, and were accepted as citizens around 1100. The family gave three Doges and numerous prelates, cardinals, magistrates and generals to the city.

The palace, which faces onto the Osmarin canal, was built at the beginning of the fourteenth century. In the 15th century the palace was extended along the San Severo canal. It is probable that the unusual and beautiful two-lancet corner windows were constructed during this time.

The window on the left, decorated with delicate openwork, probably served as a model for the windows of Ca' d'oro, constructed in 1421.

The façade facing onto the canal was completely covered with frescoes by Palma the Older, but unfortunately the frescoes have completely disappeared today.

After the fall of the Venetian Republic, the palace was divided between the Farsetti family and Mocenigo Alvisopoli family (named after Alvise Mocenigo, founder of the ideal city Alvisopoli, in the Venetian hinterland).

In his book *The stone of Venice* John Ruskin describes the palace as a typical product of Venetian Gothic Art.
Today the palace is divided into a series of apartments and cannot be visited.

Above: particular of the corner-gothic window.

Opposite: the palace on Rio dell'Osmarin.

Palazzo Priuli Ruzzini

Moving to Venice from Constantinople, the Ruzzini family first appeared a public document in 994. They were a rich family, divided into several branches and they had many properties throughout Venice.

By the end of the sixteenth century, the Ruzzini family commissioned the architect Bartolomeo Manopola to design an elegant palace for them. The palace was erected in Campo Santa Maria Formosa, one of the largest districts in the city.

According to Luca Carlevanjs, the construction of the palace probably took place after a fire in 1586 which burned down some of the family's houses.

Manopola, who paid more attention to the decorative details than to the structure, demonstrated that he had studied the designs of Serlio: the short pilasters, the spare constructional elements, the attic window buttressed by scrolls clearly derive for the teachings of the maestro.

As was typical of the era, and accurately noted by Carlevarijs, on the first floor, two coat-of-arms were placed for decoration, only to disappear in the years which followed.

The façade facing onto the Paradiso canal is a typical example of a sixteenth century façade, with lions' heads at the level of the water.

The most famous member of the family was Carlo, Ambassador to Spain, Vienna and Constantinople. Carlo had a passion for books and owned manuscripts and pictures which he kept in house in San Giobbe. He also owned a collection of paintings containing almost one hundred and seventy pictures.

In 1732, at the age of eighty, Carlo was elected Doge. He never appears to have lived in the Santa Maria Formosa palace. After the fall of the Republic, the palace was recovered by Pietro Priuli and it is said that it contained major works of art by artists such as Antonio Zanchis, Carlo Loth, Federico Carvelli and Gregorio Lazzarini. Frescoes and decorative elements over the doors by Lazzarini are still conserved here. Today after many years of neglect, the building is finally being restored.

The façade on the Campo Santa Maria Formosa.

Palazzo Querini Benzon

The palace was built in the first half of the eighteenth century, by the Querini family, it was constructed on an area occupied by an older building.

The façade is characterised by its width, given movement in the centre by a four-lancet window and the projecting balconies. The ground floor is decorated with band of marble stretching up to the base of the mezzanine windows and to the capitals of the water gate. Two string-courses in marble link the windows of the first and second floor with their respective balconies at the centre of the façade.

The building owes its fame not just to its sober architecture, but also to Countess Maria Querini Benzon, a lady of great vitality and unconventionality.

The family Benzon was of ancient origin, it is said that San Venturino, martyred in 120, and San Benzone, who lived in the same era, were also members of the Benzons family.

In 1407 the Benzon family was first registered among the Venetian nobility in 1407, and a second time in 1482.

Countess Marina created a famous literary salon here in which Ugo Foscolo, Antonio Canova, Ippolito Pindemonte, Thomas Moore, Chateubriand and Byron participated enthusiastically.

Byron met Teresa Guiccioli here, abandoning Venice for her sake.

Stendhal, another assiduous visitor to Marina's salon, wrote that the most exclusives Parisian salons rooms were "stupid and arid in comparison with that of Countess Benzon".

The countess danced half-naked with Foscolo in Piazza San Marco, in 1797, around the tree of the liberty.

It appears that one of Venice's most popular songs was inspired by her, the *Blonde in the gondola*, the music of which was composed by Simone Mayr and the words written by Antonio Lamberti.

The severe eighteenth-century façade.

Palazzo Soranzo

The two Soranzo palaces in Campo San Polo, known as the "Casa Vecchia" on the right-hand side and "Casa Nuova" on the left, would appear to break the Venetian rule which establishes that the main façade of the building usually faces onto the canal: in truth the palaces did face onto the Sant'Antonio canal, but his was eliminated in 1761, as can be noted when observing the limits of the stone flagging dating back to 1493. The palaces were linked to the square by private bridges, clearly eliminated along with the canal, are slightly but clearly curved in order to follow the curved path of the Caranto canal. This is a typical feature of the Venetian architecture, whose final purpose was to maximise the use of the building area.

The façades, today joined together by the plasterwork and by windows on the ground floor, are characterised by their medieval style and fifteenth century gothic features, in a mixture of styles often described by John Ruskin as Gothic – Venetian.

The layout of the two buildings are clearly of this type, with their open door on one side and the "pòrtego" on the first floor.

The several light windows which characterise lighten the effect on both façades are hold up by an extensive dentate cornice clad in Greek marble and embellished with polychrome marble medallions and by patera decorated with animal motifs, eagles and lions. Within the cornice of the four-lancet window on the second floor there is a medallion depicting the struggle between Hercules and a lion.

These panels were apparently carved around the middle of the 14th century specifically for the decoration of the Soranzo palace, confirming the continuity of the noble family in pursuing their past traditions and the innovation of the buildings.

The two large doors are surmounted by two sculpted friezes in Romanesque style. The façade of the second building has an eight-lancet window on the first floor. It was richly decorated with frescoes by Giorgione which have disappeared entirely today.

The Soranzos family gave the Venetian Republic sixteen magistrates of San Marco.

Doge Giovanni Soranzo, a sea captain who conquered the Genovese at Caffa, welcomed Dante Aligheri, who had arrived in Venice in the role of Ambassador for the Polenta family, Lords of Ravenna, to his palace in around 1320.

The façade on Campo San Polo.

Palazzo Soranzo van Axel

The palace defined as a *Domus Magna* in the act of sale, originally belonged to the Grandenigo family and was purchased on November 27, 1473, by the attorney of San Marco, Nicolò Soranzo, for the notable sum of four thousand golden ducats. The pre-existing Byzantine building, traces of which remain in the pateras, the medallions and the cornice on the first floor, was immediately subjected to radical intervention and the new palace was completed in 1479. The layout and the front views are particularly unusual, firstly because the palace is divided into two, each unit with rooms designed for two different families, and also because the configuration of the area strongly conditioned the regularity of the construction. There are therefore two entrances, both from land and water, two courtyards, two staircases, two wells and obviously two façades. One façade faces onto the Panada canal, while the other looks out over the San Canciano canal, with two three-lancet windows in the centre, while the halls are not straight but bent at an angle. At the bottom of the

foundation, one of the two land entrances is found: the monumental ogival door is, according to Ruskin: "the only completely intact monumental door in Venice, having conserved the richly carved wooden shutter, with a spy-hole to observe and a door knocker in the shape of a fish" and it is embellished with an dentate cornice terminating with pendentive which frames the Van Axel coat-of-arms, which was added in the sixteenth century. From here we can reach internal court which has preserved the florid gothic features, with the ground floor arcades and the staircase, one of the most interesting from the late fifteenth century in Venice. The importance of the courtyard is emphasised by the architectural importance of the external staircase, perfectly conserved, which makes its way at monumental pace, with a balustrade with small columns and trefoil arches decorated with small human heads made of Istria stone.
The emotional impact of this place is further increased by the Venetian – Byzantine, Gothic and Renaissance decorative elements which

seem to echo the 16th century well curb. The palace remained the property of the Soranzo family for almost two centuries, until the 1599. Then it came into the hands of Alvise Venier, a man of culture and poet much praised by Pietro Aretino and also an important political figure. In 1628 it was sold by Alvise's heirs to Matteo Sanuto. Finally in 1652 the whole palace was acquired by the Van Axels, Flemish merchants who joined the Venetian nobility in 1665 in return for payment. The Van Axels opened the rooms to high society, as on the occasion of the wedding of Giovanni Battista to Margherita Bembo in 1665, or when they entertained the Duke of Brunswick – Wolfenbuttel in the palace. In 1920 the building was acquired by the antique antiquarian Dino Barozzi, who carried out delicate restoration work.

The façade on la Panada canal.

Pages 190-191: the inside court keeps the original fifteenth-century typology with the uncovered staircase, the arcade and the well-curb.

Palazzo Venier dei Leoni

The powerful and rich Venier family, which gave the Venetian Republic three Doges and a series of magistrates of San Marco, lived in the Dorsoduro in the area of Campo San Vios and the church " della Salute" in a big gothic palace known as the "Torresella" palace, due to the square tower, in truth not particularly small, which overlooked it and which can be recognised in eighteenth century views of Venice(particularly those by Canaletto).

The Venier family decided to have a more important residence constructed on the site of the old and by then dilapidated building. The intention was to outdo the neighbouring Palazzo Ca' Granda belonging to the Corner family.

In 1740 the Venier entrusted construction of the palace to the architect Lorenzo Boschetti, who planned an imposing and monumental structure, of considerable depth (which can still be appreciate it in the wood model on display in the Correr Museum).

The construction of the building, whether for financial or other reasons is not known, was interrupted at the first floor and was never continued. Hence the ground floor was completed and covered in Istria stone, despite its incomplete nature highlighting the marked characteristics unmistakably recalling Sansoviani and Longhenian motifs, with its large wide stairway leading to the entrance, marked by imposing pilasters truncated at the level of the arches. The stunted building known as the "mai finio"(never finished), with it's romantic and luxuriant rear garden, probably owes its real name to the fact that the Venier kept an African Lion there in a cage.

The palace was subsequently purchased by the rich and eccentric American art collector Peggy Guggenheim, who made it into a museum of contemporary art as well as her residence.

Guggenheim died in 1979 and the palace remained the property of the Solomon R. Guggenheim foundation in New York, which now uses it exclusively as a museum. Among the many important works of modern art displayed here there are sculptures and pictures by Piccasso, Braque, Max Ernst; Klee, De Chirico, Pollock, Marino Marini, Alexander Calder and Giacometti, as well as by Venetian artists who participated in this last artistic salon within the city, Trancedi, Bepi Santomaso and Emilio Vedova.

The Istria's stone basement, the only built part of the eighteenth-century palace.

Page 194: sculpture of Luciano Minguzzi in the inside garden.

Page 195: sculpture of Marino Marini placed in axis with the entrance of the water.

Page 196: the window of Peggy Guggenheim's sleeping-room.

Bibliography

ARSLAN E., *Venezia gotica*, Electa Editore, Venezia 1970

AUGUSTI A., *Ca' d'Oro. La galleria Giorgio Franchetti*, Electa Editore, Milano 1998

BASSI E., *Architettura del sei e settecento a Venezia*, Filippi Editre, Venezia 1980

BASSI E., *Palazzi di Venezia*, La Stamperia di Venezia Editrice, Venezia 1976

BETTINI S., *Venezia nascita di una città*, Electa Editore, Milano 1988

CALABI D., MORACCHIELLO P., *Rialto le fabbriche e il ponte*, Einaudi, Torino 1987

CONCINA E., *Storia dell'architettura di Venezia*, Electa, Milano 1995

CRISTINELLI, G., *Baldassarre Longhena*, Marsilio Editori, Padova 1972

CUNACCIA C. M., *Interni a Venezia*, Arsenale Editrice, Venezia 1994

DELL'ORSO C., *Venezia libertina*, Arsenale Editrice, Venezia 1999

DEL MAR J., *Indicatore anagrafico di Venezia*, Libreria Sansovino, Venezia 1996

FASOLO J., *Un'altra Venezia*, Arsenale Editrice, Venezia 2000

FONTANA G., *Venezia monumentale. I palazzi*, Venezia 1967

FRANZOI U., *Canal Grande*, Arsenale Editrice, Venezia 1993

IKEDA D., *La nuova rivoluzione umana*, Esperia Edizioni, Milano 2001

LORENZETTI G., *Venezia e il suo estuario*, Roma 1956

MARETTO P., *La casa veneziana nella storia della città*, Marsilio Editori, Venezia 1986

MC ANDREW J., *L'architettura veneziana del primo Rinascimento*, Marsilio Editori, Venezia 1995

PEDROCCO F., *Ca' Rezzonico. Museo del Settecento veneziano*, Marsilio Editori, Venezia 2001

PIAMONTE G., *Venezia vista dall'acqua*, La Stamperia di Venezia Editrice, Venezia 1992

PUPPI L., OLIVATO PUPPI L., *Mauro Codussi*, Electa, Milano 1977

RIZZO T., *I ponti di Venezia*, Newton Compton Editori, Roma 1998

ROMANELLI G., *Ritratto di Venezia*, Arsenale Editrice, Venezia 1996

ROSSI A., *L'architettura della città*, Città Studi, Milano 1991.

RUSKIN J., *Le pietre di Venezia*, A. Mondadori Ed., Milano 1981

RUSSO R., *Palazzi di Venezia*, Arsenale Editrice, Venezia 1998

SCANNAPIECO A., *Casa di Carlo Goldoni*, Marsilio Editori, Venezia 2001

SCOTTON F., *Ca' Pesaro. Galleria internazionale d'arte moderna*, Marsilio Editori, Venezia 2002

SELVATICO, P., *Sull'architettura e sulla scultura in Venezia*, Arnoldo Forni Editore, Sala Bolognese 1980

TAFURI M., *Venezia e il Rinascimento*, Einaudi, Torino 1985

TASSINI G., *Curiosità veneziane*, Filippi Editore, Venezia 1970

TOSO FEI A., *Leggende veneziane e storie di fantasmi*, Editrice Elzeviro, Treviso 2002

ZORZI A., *Canal Grande*, Rizzoli, Milano 1991

ZORZI A., *I palazzi veneziani*, Magnus Edizioni, Udine 1989

ZORZI A., *Venezia scomparsa*, Electa, Milano 1984

ZUCCONI G., *Venezia guida all'architettura*, Arsenale Editrice, Venezia 1993

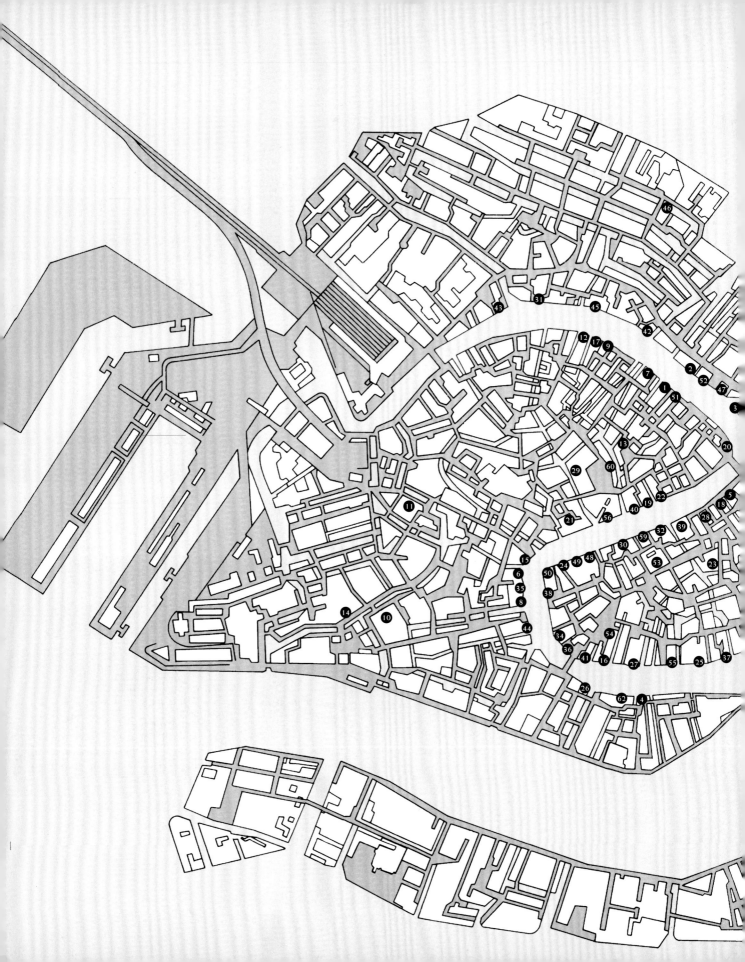

1-Ca' Corner della Regina
2-Ca' d'Oro
3-Ca' Da Mosto
4-Ca' Dario
5-Ca' Dolfin Manin
6-Ca' Foscari
7-Ca' Pesaro
8-Ca' Rezzonico
9-Ca' Tron
10-Ca' Zenobio
11-Casa Torres
12-Fondaco dei Turchi
13-Palazzo Albrizzi
14-Palazzo Ariani
15-Palazzo Balbi
16-Palazzo Barbaro
17-Palazzo Belloni Battagia
18-Palazzo Bembo
19-Palazzo Bernardo
20-Palazzo dei Camerlenghi
21-Palazzo Centani
22-Palazzo Coccina Tiepolo Papadopoli
23-Palazzo Contarini del Bovolo
24-Palazzo Contarini delle Figure
25-Palazzo Contarini Fasan
26-Palazzo Contarini Dal Zaffo
27-Palazzo Corner della Ca' Granda
28-Palazzo Corner Loredan Piscopia
29-Palazzo Corner-Mocenigo
30-Palazzo Corner Spinelli
31-Palazzo Correr Contarini Zorzi
32-Palazzo d'Anna
33-Palazzo Dandolo
34-Palazzo Falier Canossa
35-Palazzo Giustinian
36-Palazzo Giustinian Lolin
37-Palazzo Giustinian Morosini
38-Palazzo Grassi
39-Palazzo Griman
40-Palazzo Grimani Marcello
41-Palazzo Gussoni Cavalli Franchetti
42-Palazzo Gussoni Grimani Della Vida
43-Palazzo Labia
44-Palazzo Loredan dell'Ambasciatore
45-Palazzo Loredan Vendramin Calergi
46-Palazzo Mastelli del Cammello
47-Palazzo Michiel delle Colonne
48-Palazzo Mocenigo Casa Nuova
49-Palazzo Mocenigo Casa Vecchia
50-Palazzo Moro-Lin
51-Palazzo Morosini Brandolini
52-Palazzo Morosini Sagredo
53-Palazzo Pesaro degli Orfei, Fortuny
54-Palazzo Pisani
55-Palazzo Pisani Gritti
56-Palazzo Pisani Moretta
57-Palazzo Priuli all'Osmarin
58-Palazzo Priuli Ruzzini
59-Palazzo Querini Benzon
60-Palazzo Soranzo
61-Palazzo Soranzo van Axel
62-Palazzo Venier dei Leoni